For the
Love
of God

For the Love of God

THE BIBLE AS AN OPEN BOOK

Alicia Suskin Ostriker

Rutgers University Press

New Brunswick, New Jersey, and London

Library of Congress Cataloging-in-Publication Data

Ostriker, Alicia.

  For the love of God : the Bible as an open book / Alicia Suskin Ostriker.

    p. cm.

  Includes bibliographical references.

  ISBN-13: 978-0-8135-4200-3 (hardcover : alk. paper)

  1. Bible and feminism. 2. Bible and literature. 3. Feminism—Religious aspects—Judaism.

4. Bible. O.T.—Criticism, interpretation, etc. I. Title.

  BS680.W70875 2007

  221.6'082—dc22

2007005965

A British Cataloging-in-Publication record for this book is available from the British Library.

Visit our Web site: http://rutgerspress.rutgers.edu

Manufactured in the United States of America

For Abigail and Naomi

blessed in your goings out and your comings in

Contents

T he present book continues the labor and pleasure of wrestling with the Jewish Bible and Jewish tradition, a task I began in 1985. The story of that beginning is told in *The Nakedness of the Fathers: Biblical Visions and Revisions,* a combination of prose and poetry, midrash and autobiography, re-imagining biblical stories from Genesis to Job and beyond. A quite different sort of book is *Feminist Revision and the Bible,* published first but begun second, in part as an attempt to find a context for the unconventionality of *Nakedness*—an unconventionality new to me at the time, but which I later came to understand as widely shared. The Bible is itself the most subversive and boundary-breaking of texts, not least because it is so full of contradiction and because it both rejects and invites challenges to authority. The two lectures that form the heart of *Feminist Revision and the Bible* were given at Bucknell College, as one of the annual Bucknell lectures in Literary Theory.

In 2002 I published a volume of poems, *The Volcano Sequence,* which in a sense picked up where *Nakedness* left off, recording a piecemeal attempt to locate the Divine in my own life and in the life of my society. It seems to me that our images of a Father God are responsible for much human suffering, some of which might be ameliorated if we had equal access to his repressed or submerged female self, whose name in Kabbala, the tradition of Jewish mysticism, is the Shekhinah. The question of the Shekhina is central to these poems, as is the question of repressed anger and its consequences.

For the Love of God: The Bible as an Open Book approaches the Bible from a more wide-angle lens. Troubled by the way the Bible has become synonymous in our culture with a moralizing authoritarianism, I wanted to look at some of its most unconventional and outrageous portions, in order to make clear how amazingly heterogeneous they are, as well as how much they tell us about the lives we are living and the world in which we live. I do believe that the Bible asks to be taken both personally and analytically. If not taken personally, it becomes meaningless; if not taken analytically, it becomes dogma. But the consequences of taking the Song of Songs, the Book of Ruth, Psalms, Ecclesiastes, Jonah, and Job both personally and analytically are startling, as I discovered in the course of writing.

The chapters on the Song of Songs and Ruth both emerge from a feminist perspective, but they carry that perspective forward in different directions. The chapter on Psalms was a response to the destruction of the World Trade Center Towers in New York City. Understanding Ecclesiastes involved an effort to see what the spark of joy in this most pessimistic book was all about. The story of Jonah, read on the Day of Atonement, is of profound psychological and political import, today as well as in ancient times. My chapter on Job, the biblical text that originally impelled me on this journey, is a fresh attempt to understand what the Hebrew Bible, and Jewish tradition growing out of it, makes of a One God who is responsible for both good and evil. I believe that each of these books has something to say about the Being we call God, but no two say the same thing. That is a deeply satisfying fact. At any rate, it is satisfying to me as a Jew. For Jewish tradition tells us that "there is always another interpretation." I write in the hope that my readers will feel free to engage in their own interpretive acts.

Work such as this is essentially collective, and I am grateful to many friends and associates for their stimulating and wise conversations, criticisms, and suggestions. Jill Hammer, J. Cheryl Exum, Mary Campbell, Athalya Brenner, Diana Lipton, Chana Bloch, Yvonne Sherwood, Sheila Solomon, Michael Venditozzi, and Peter Pitzele have all clarified my thinking. Harold Schweizer, Barry Qualls, Arthur Waskow, Gerald Stern, C. K. Williams, Arthur Strimling, and Eric Selinger have encouraged me to remember that I am not alone, that many others are engaged in the enterprise of re-imagining our sacred texts and traditions. My Rutgers University students and the participants in my midrash writing workshops have expanded my imagination. My husband, J. P. Ostriker, reading multiple versions, has consistently improved my prose. I appreciate as well the semesters spent on academic leave from Rutgers and the weeks spent at the MacDowell colony; both respites enabled me to read and write intensively.

Regarding translations: I have relied on the King James Version (KJV) in my chapters on the Song of Songs, Psalms, and Job, for the sake of its beauty as well as its high degree of faithfulness to the Hebrew.[1] For Ruth, Ecclesiastes, and Jonah I have consulted the KJV along with several modern versions, including the Revised Standard Version, the New Revised Standard Version, and the 1999 Jewish Publication Society translations. Here my intention is to convey the brisk quality of the biblical prose in a manner that feels relatively modern, using "you" for second-person singular pronouns and avoiding other conspicuous archaisms. The reader who is without Hebrew should feel free to travel like a bee among multiple translations, collecting verbal pollen, just as one might do with translations of Baudelaire or Li Po. As parallax determines the location of celestial bodies, diverse translations can be useful in determining meaning.

Grateful acknowledgment is made to the following for permission to reprint:

The lines by Alta beginning "I felt the joy" are from "Putting It All Down in Black & White," from *The Shameless Hussy: Selected Stories, Essays and Poems* (Crossing Press, 1980); the lines from Rumi beginning "I've heard it said," translated by Coleman Barks are from *Open Secret: Versions of Rumi* (Threshold Books, 1984); the lines from "Sex Without Love" by Sharon Olds, are from *the Dead and the Living* (New York: Knopf, 1983); Yehuda Amichai, "God Has Pity," is from *The Selected Poems,* translated by Chana Bloch and Stephen Mitchell (New York: Harper & Row, 1986); Amichai, "When I Die," from *Open Closed Open,* translated by Chana Bloch and Chana Kronenfeld (New York: Harcourt, 2000). Poems quoted from Alicia Ostriker, *The Volcano Sequence* (University of Pittsburgh Press, 2002) by permission of the author. Several passages in "Job: the Open Book" are taken from Alicia Suskin Ostriker, *The Nakedness of the Fathers: Biblical Visions and Revisions* (Rutgers University Press, 1994). Previous versions of "Song of Songs" appeared in *The Song of Songs: A Feminist Companion to the Bible, Second Series* edited by Athalya Brenner and Carole R. Fontaine (Sheffield, Eng.: Sheffield Academic Press, 2000); "The Book of Ruth and the Love of the Land," in *Biblical Interpretation* 10.4. 2002; "Psalm and Anti-Psalm" in *American Poetry Review* July–August 2002; "Ecclesiastes" in *American Poetry Review* Jan.–Feb. 2005; "Jonah" in *Georgia Review* Summer 2005; "Job" in *Michigan Quarterly Review, Spring 2007.*

For the
Love
of God

INTRODUCTION

Sing unto the Lord a new song.

—PSALM 96.1

hen we awaken, we open our eyes. When we love, we open our hearts and arms. When we think, we open our minds. Most of us like to feel that we are open to life, that we do not want to leave it before we have lived it. To say that the Bible is an open book is to say that anyone may read it, that any one may enter its chapter and verse. It is there for us, for all to see. But to call the Bible open is also to say that it encourages awakening, loving, thinking, and being more alive.

This is neither the usual picture of scripture nor its usual function. Scripture is supposed to be boring, full of begats; or a text used to regulate people's behavior and suppress their enjoyment of life; or something to *save* them from living; or something tyrannical; or something simply passé. To its enemies, scripture represents the worst of the past: it is deeply and stubbornly retrograde in matters sexual, scientific, and of course political. Because the world's culture wars and shooting wars are commonly religious wars—or political conflicts disguised as religious—scripture is enlisted to support inflexible agendas in the name of God, by people who feel certain that God shares their opinions. How do they know? In America in the twenty-first century, as a rule, they know because they "read the Bible." But how much of the Bible do they read? Are they aware that the same Good Book that sanctions war has a chapter that questions the goodness of God? And another that celebrates unmarried sex?

Our society seems to be wedded to the Bible, for better or worse. But to a highly selective set of texts, not to the *whole* Bible. Those selected texts, it is assumed, all have the same basic messages to give us, about faith and obedience to authority, about the soul, and sex, and sin, and salvation. God is merciful if you repent your sins but will punish you if you don't. He requires submission and worship. If your people have enemies, then he is a man of war. He is primarily a judge. Such ideas are tightly woven into the fabric of the being we call God the Father. For believers and nonbelievers alike, the Bible stands as the quintessential source of dogma and authority in society. Many Americans consider it more authoritative than either the legal system or scientific knowledge. Yet an extraordinary wealth of alternative ideas and possibilities exists, scattered throughout the biblical texts—ideas and possibilities that either question divine authority, or re-define it, or ignore it altogether.

The biblical scholar and translator Robert Alter observes that scripture incorporates radically diverse conceptions "of history, ethics, psychology . . . of priesthood and laity, Israel and the nations, even of God."[1] I like to couple this description with one of the sayings about Torah in *Pirke Avot,* the Ethics of the Fathers: "Turn it and turn it, for everything is in it." Although Alter's statement comes from a tradition of secular literary criticism and *Pirke Avot's* from within a strictly religious tradition, they share the perception that the Bible is not a set of dogmas teaching the same lesson over and over *ad infinitum,* but a treasury of plural possibilities.

If we remember that the Hebrew Bible was composed by multiple (mostly anonymous) authors during a period of about one thousand years—something like the time between Beowulf and T. S. Eliot—and compiled and edited during another four hundred or so, it is not surprising that scripture is a wildly composite set of documents, an arena of mysteries, gaps, and inconsistencies. We can find in it dogma and resistance to dogma, faith and submission but also doubt and challenge, law and subversion of law, promises of safety and meaning but also assurances of utter chaos. Sublimity, but also comedy. The abstract and the deliciously sensuous. A Father God, certainly, but also hints, here and there, of the Divine Mother who was edited out of historical memory.

"The past is not dead," William Faulkner remarked in his Nobel Prize speech; "it is not even past." Scripture is deeply archaic and starkly contemporary, universalist and tribal, conservative and radical, personal and public, hotly physical and coolly metaphysical. It can and should yield nourishment to many different sorts of hunger. The Bible's irreducible excess, its contradictoriness, its multiplicity, make it dazzling and durable as literature; it might also be said that these qualities point toward the irreducible plenitude and unknowability of God.

King Solomon, dedicating the temple he has just finished constructing in Jerusalem, offers a prayer that contains one of the most remarkable and moving lines in all the Bible. "Behold," he says to the Holy One, "the heaven of heavens cannot contain thee; how much less this house that I have builded" (1 Kings 8.27). Here is a sentence I should like to see inscribed on the forehead of every literalist and fundamentalist on earth—Jewish, Christian, Muslim—everyone who has the arrogance to believe that we human beings, specks of dust that we are in the cosmos, have plumbed the depths of God's meaning. Have pinned down the Maker. Caged the Creator. I remember encountering this sentence for the first time a half century ago, during the summer of my junior year in college, when I had made it my project to read through the Old Testament from beginning to end. The deeper significance of these words thrilled me; it still does. Today, I try to imagine the change in the global religious climate if literalist and fundamentalist readers of every stripe should come to understand that the petty structures of our intellects, theologies, and dogmas can never contain God.

I try to imagine, as well, the change in global politics. King Solomon is described as the wisest man on earth. The sublimity and humility of his prayer correlates with what is known of his reign. Whereas his father David was a warrior all his life, Solomon, whose Hebrew name *Shlomo* is a cognate of *Shalom,* peace, engaged in treaties and trade with his neighbors. We need this sort of wisdom in our rulers; we need a God who can encourage fewer crusades, jihads, occupations, massacres, and assassinations, and more treaties; a God whose primary metaphors are not hierarchical, imperialistic, and dualistic; a God to help us survive the nuclear age.[2]

This book is an attempt to understand some of the wildest, strangest, most splendid writing in western tradition: what it means to me personally, what it might mean to us collectively. I write about the Bible as a woman, a Jew, and a poet. I write about the Hebrew Bible because it is my heritage. The men and women in it are my mothers and fathers. Anywhere I look, it offers a mirror of myself. It seems to want me to live more intensely. It is sexual and skeptical, just as I am. It illuminates the fractured and violent world in which I live with horrifying force. It also points, on occasion, to something closer to the heart's desire. This makes it fascinating as a puzzle, or an intricate set of puzzles. And, of course, I read and write about the Bible because the texts are infinitely rich, provocative, various, and beautiful, so that to read is happiness, and to attempt interpretation is a further happiness. For the more one looks, the more one sees.

The set of biblical texts I am exploring here seems to me a sort of fireworks display, with rockets shooting off in multiple shimmering directions. That is what gives the feeling of openness. Each is what I call a countertext, by which I mean a text that deviates from particular dominant biblical concepts and motifs, thereby enriching and deepening the Bible as a whole.[3] I begin with the melting eroticism of the Song of Songs, a poem in celebration of sex outside of marriage. Readers coming to the Song of Songs for the first time commonly express astonishment at its apparently sacrilegious presence in scripture; God is never mentioned once in it; yet the great rabbi Akiba declared the Song "a holy of holies." By both Jews and Christians, the Song has been interpreted as a sacred text. What happens if we imagine that the Beloved in this poem is actually God? The Book of Ruth, which I look at next, also centers around love, and is profoundly woman-centered, but here we see a turn toward political issues. Why is it that this story could take place only in peacetime? How is it that the most famous passage in Ruth is used in gay wedding ceremonies? And what does it mean that Ruth, a Moabite woman, is to become the great-grandmother of King David? My third chapter, written in response to the destruction of the World Trade Center in 2001, looks at Psalms as devotional poems magnificently exploring the individual's intimate need of relationship with God—but also as developing a magnificent rhetoric in support of holy war. The world of Psalms is filled with "enemies," "sinners," "the wicked," whom God is exhorted to punish. How should we respond to the fact that the language of many psalms so closely resembles the language of Islamic jihad?

In my fourth chapter, I suggest that the Book of Jonah asks a question that goes to the heart of international politics in the twenty-first century, but implies an answer very different from that of Psalms. With Jonah, it appears to me, we see a striking representation of how hatred of the Self and hatred of the Other are two sides of a single psychic coin. In another kind of contrast, in Ecclesiastes, a personal relationship with God is represented as manifestly impossible, and the author sounds like something of a crypto-Buddhist. Finally, when we reach the Book of Job, where anything that has ever been felt about the cosmic injustice of the world finds its eloquent voice, the goodness of the Holy One is definitively challenged.

These writings, individually and collectively, are astonishing. Far from conveying a single message or representing a consistent view of what we are doing when we love God, these books deviate radically from one another as well as from any "normative" view. The ground they cover is immense. The interpretations in the following chapters are examples of how one contemporary reader responds to this open book at the beginning of the twenty-first century. They are not designed to be prescriptive. With luck, readers will instantly begin interpreting for themselves. My title, *For the Love of God,* points two ways: it can be either an utterance of explosive exasperation, or one of devotion. When Moses at Sinai begs God, "'Oh, let me behold your Presence,'" he is told, "'You cannot see my face, for man cannot see me and live.'" But he is also told,

> "See, there is a place near me. Station yourself on the
> rock and as my Presence passes by, I will place you in
> a cleft of the rock and shield you with my hand until

I have passed by. Then I will take my hand away and
you will see my back; but my face cannot be seen."
(Exodus 33.18–23)

The imagery is suggestively both sexual and mystical. I believe that the "back" of God, whose beauty and terror would
destroy us at close quarters, may be apprehended through
the hints, indirections, and subtleties of poetry and storytelling. These images, these gestures, these metaphors. We see
through a glass darkly, as St. Paul says. The Song of Songs, the
Book of Ruth, Psalms, Jonah, Ecclesiastes, and Job can lead
us, at least, to know that there are many ways of seeing—and
many ways of seeing that immaterial elephant-in-the-room,
God, *Adonai, Elohim, El Shaddai,* the One who in Kabbala is
Ein Sof, the Endless One.

We are told that Torah is a tree of life to those who take
hold of it. A tree branches in many directions. That is one
difference between a tree and a dry stick. When Aaron's rod
flowers, it becomes a true emblem of the spirit. When it is
merely a rod, it represents *halakha,* the strict laws that may
be necessary to sustain a community through adversity over
years and centuries, diaspora, pogrom and shoah; but a rod is
not alive. We know that a tree is alive because it grows. Inch
by persistent inch its twigs extend themselves, the buds press
forth, open into sheer green mist, thicken into foliage, wither
and fall—and the twigs inch outward another season. We
are mandated, in Jewish tradition, to keep interpreting and
reinterpreting Torah until the end of time; we are told that all
interpretations were already foreknown by God at Sinai; we
are told that "there is always another interpretation" and that
every interpretation becomes a part of the ever-growing tree.
It is my hope, in this book, to add a twig or leaflet to this

foliage. A greater hope is that others will do as I have done: read the Bible not as they have been officially taught, but for themselves, with their own eyes and minds. May they read for joy and personal illumination, may they read with compassion for human suffering, may they read for the love of God.

THE SONG OF SONGS:
A HOLY OF HOLIES

I felt the joy of being a body,

of being inside a body, of

another body being inside my

body; the unbearable joy

— ALTA

he Song of Songs is a book overwhelmingly about joy. "Let him kiss me with the kisses of his mouth; for thy love is better than wine" is its famous opening. With this pronoun-blurring sentence we are plunged into a breathlessly seductive and ultimately mysterious love scene. The remainder of the Song is essentially an erotic sequence of lyric dialogues between two young lovers who yearn for, recall, invite, and celebrate each other's caresses in language ripe with metaphors that are both explicit and cryptic, and that seem to have triggered endless scholarly debates about their meaning.

The poem's location is a world of fertile nature into which the lovers seem to blend as they volley their images back and forth:

I am the Rose of Sharon, and the lily of the valleys. As the lily among thorns, so is my love among the daughters. As the apple tree among the trees of the wood, so is my beloved among the sons. I sat down under his

shadow with great delight, and his fruit was sweet to
my taste. (2.2–4)

Or it is the sumptuous fantasied setting of a royal court,
interchangeable with a male body:

His hands are as gold rings set with the beryl: his belly
is as bright ivory overlaid with sapphires. His legs are as
pillars of marble, set upon sockets of fine gold. (5.14–15)

The man is sometimes a shepherd, sometimes a king,
while the woman is at times an enclosed garden, at times a
princess, at times "my myrrh with my spice . . . my honeycomb
with my honey . . . my wine with my milk" (5.1). The lovers
are sometimes alone, sometimes accompanied by friends. Neither is named, although the woman is once referred to as the
Shulamite, which may mean "woman from Jerusalem" or possibly "woman of peace" or "Solomon's woman"; some commentators have taken the name to mean "woman from Shunam,"
which is the birthplace of the biblical Abishag, a woman famous for her beauty.

The man at one moment seems to be playing the role
of King Solomon, and at another to be scorning Solomon's
wealth as inferior to the vineyard of his beloved's body. He
calls her "my sister, my bride," although it is clear that they
are neither siblings nor married; they call each other beloved
and friend; they compare each other to doves, deer, a mare, a
wild stag. An elliptical refrain that occurs for the first time
during a scene of lovemaking, "He brought me to the ban-
queting house, and his banner over me was love . . . His left
hand is under my head, and his right hand doth embrace me"
(2.4–6), reinforces the imagery of love as belonging to a fruitful natural world:

I charge you, O ye daughters of Jerusalem, by the roes,
and by the hinds of the field, that ye stir not up, nor
awake my love, till he please. (2.7, 3.5, 8.4)

An alternative translation of this ambiguous line is "stir
not up nor awaken love until it please." Or "until it wishes."
Whether it is the young man in particular who is not to be
awakened, or whether it is "love" itself, that needs to be protected until it ripens on its own, or whether the Shulamite
is urgently advising her friends about their own future love
lives, this tender warning is unique in the Bible.

I sat down to read the poem for the first time when I was
in my teens, for an English class. I had no trouble understanding it. The unutterably sweet words seemed to come not from
outside but from inside myself, as if my most intimate truths
were projected onto the screen of the page. I was sixteen, in
love with a boy two years older, whose eyes and laugh and body
were so beautiful to me that they appeared to contain and en-
close the stars, and the spaces between the stars. He stood with
the grace of trees. His face reflected my joy, his arms cherished
me and made me safe as a lamb. Our kisses were sweet, play-
ful, intense, almost unbearable, just right. Whatever parts of
the poem I didn't understand, it didn't matter. I understood
the tone. Meeting and parting, parting and meeting—in love
and playing at love, in a state of entire confidence.

But how is it, contemporary readers tend to ask, that the
Song of Songs came to be included in the Bible? What is this
most erotic sequence of poems doing in sacred scripture? The
question is an ancient one, and it raises the larger question of
what we mean—or might mean—by "sacredness," by "scripture," and by "the erotic."

Let me make several suggestions. First: the love cele-
brated in the Song may be understood as equally natural and

spiritual. It is no accident that Jewish, Christian, Sufi and Hindu mystics all speak of God as the beloved and that everyone in love sees the beloved's face as holy. If elsewhere we must divide the "sacred" from the "secular," that division is annihilated in the Song. Here, for once, it becomes meaningless. In addition, the Song is extraordinary not only because of its sexual content but because its poetic structure and language imply alternatives to our usual modes of perceiving and categorizing reality, and especially to the usual biblical modes of classifying things. Experiencing the Song as an image of possible human relationship leads us, besides, to a new image of our relationship with God. Finally, I want to suggest that 5.2–8, a uniquely painful episode in the Song, may be read as a poem of women's spiritual yearning, our exclusion by tradition, and a plea for inclusion that appeals not only to desire but also to justice.

Torah: What's Love Got to Do With It

How did the Song of Songs come to be included in the Bible? To this question we have speculation but no precise answer.[1] We know that a debate occurred over the Song's inclusion, for we have two famous quotations from Rabbi Akiva (d. 135 CE) on the topic. "No man in Israel," he is supposed to have exclaimed over the heads of a dubious rabbinical committee, "ever disputed the status of the Song of Songs. . . . The whole world is not worth the day on which the Song of Songs was given to Israel, for all the writings are holy, but the Song of Songs is the Holy of Holies." To Akiva also, however, is attributed the following warning: "He who trills his voice in chanting the Song of Songs in the banquet house, treating it as an ordinary song, has no part in the world to come."[2]

This tells us that in the same epoch as the Song was declared sacred, worthy of being part of the Bible, it was declared off-limits for a secular interpretation.

The text of the Song has been construed in rabbinic commentary for two thousand years as an allegory of the love between God and Israel, or as a coded narrative of Israel's covenantal history, or as a symbolic evocation of the soul's yearning. Christian commentary has taken it to represent the love of Christ for the Church, or for the individual Christian soul, or the "mystical marriage" of God and the Virgin Mary. Both Jewish and Christian mystical writings have been deeply indebted to its representations of longing and ecstasy. Only within the last century has the Song of Songs been widely read as a secular love poem.

Still, today's reader may wonder whether the official allegorical white-out has ever quite blotted the poetry's sensuousness from the hearts of its singers, readers, and interpreters. Akiva's admonition informs us that the Song must indeed have been sung in taverns, with or without theological approval; and every rabbinical protest that the Song is *not* to be understood in its "simple" sense seems to confirm that it inevitably *was* so understood. The traditional attribution of support for the Song to Akiva is interesting because Akiva is himself a romantically pastoral figure in Jewish legend, an unlettered shepherd loved by the landowner's daughter, yet he is also our preeminent mystic, able to ascend to the divine worlds and remain unharmed. Like the Song, he bridges the realms of body and spirit. Late in the first century CE, the Mishnah recounts that on the fifteenth of Av and the Day of Atonement, unmarried girls of Jerusalem would dress in white and go out to the vineyards to dance and sing for prospective husbands, chanting verses from the Book of Proverbs and the Song of Songs.[3] This suggests that Jews in ancient times were less inclined to differentiate between spiritual and bodily love than we are. Perhaps it suggests that they regarded Israel's survival— dependent in the postexilic era on bodily love, which alone could guarantee posterity—as itself sacred.

"A poem about erotic love would seem out of place in Holy Scripture," Chana Bloch remarks in the introduction to her and Ariel Bloch's translation of the Song, "if one's point of reference is the antipathy to sexuality in the New Testament. But sex is no sin in the Old Testament."[4] On the contrary, the Hebrew Bible tends to support the joining of man and woman in "one flesh" along with other bodily satisfactions, and indeed to see all bodily functions as potentially sacramental, in ways that remain influential throughout the future course of Judaism. In his book *Carnal Israel,* Daniel Boyarin analyzes Talmudic endorsements of marriage and sexuality as God-given, persuasively arguing that the encrusted body-spirit dualism of western thought originally derives from Hellenistic rather than ancient Judaic culture.[5] Within Jewish mysticism, sexual symbolism is not occasional but pervasive; the Oneness of God is androgynous, and the wedded state is the human ideal. "When is a man called complete in his resemblance to the Supernal?" asks the Zohar, the thirteenth-century mystical text that is the foundation stone of Kabbala. "When he couples with his spouse in oneness, joy and pleasure."[6] Raphael Patai reminds us that Lurianic Kabbalists welcomed the Sabbath Bride with words from the Song of Songs and believed it a *mitzvah* to embrace their wives on Sabbath eve: "On Friday after midnight a man should make love with his wife, saying 'I fulfill the commandment of copulation for the unification of the Holy one, blessed be He, and the Shekhinah.'" As Patai somewhat coyly notes, "the scriptural libretto for those proceedings in which earthlings emulated and stimulated the divine bride and groom . . . was, and continues to be, most appropriately, the Sublime Song of Love ascribed to Solomon, who is renowned for his zeal and devotion in this way of worship."[7] According to 1 Kings 11.13, Solomon had seven hundred wives and three hundred concubines, which might well have helped make him the wisest man on earth. A charming corollary is the Hassidic story of the student who hid under his rabbi's bed and heard him chatting and laughing while making love with his wife. However exceptional the tale, there is something quintessentially Jewish in its mix of comedy, spirituality, and the erotic: when his master discovered his presence and tried to chase him away, the disciple replied, "It is Torah and I must learn it."[8]

Does it make sense to suppose that the Song celebrates a sensuality and sexuality initially understood as simultaneously human and divine? The origins of this poem remain mysterious. Conventionally attributed to King Solomon, commentators have dated it anywhere between the tenth and the second century BCE. It may have been written in part or altogether by a woman or women, if, as has been claimed, women were professional singers and songmakers in the Ancient Near East.[9] Its praise of body parts in metaphoric lists is a device in Persian poetry. Its pastoral setting and some of its phrases recall the idylls of Theocritus and the Hellenistic genre of pastoral love poetry. The Song may be a set of popular wedding-songs, it may derive from fertility rituals (despite the fact that the lovers are evidently unmarried and that their joy in each other's embraces has to do with pleasure not progeny), and it may stem from as far back as Sumerian poems celebrating the sacred marriage of the Sumerian goddess Innanna, "queen of the universe," and her consort Dumuzi, in the third millennium BCE, or from the Babylonian cult of Ishtar-Tammuz. It has strong parallels in Tamil love poetry and in the Gita-Govinda as well as Ancient Near Eastern poetry.[10] In all these traditions, love between gods is a model for ideal love between men and women. As above, so below.

Many people, both Jews and Christians, may assume that sexual codes within Judaism have always been simple and rigid, but the foremost Jewish feminist theologian of our time, Judith Plaskow, argues that Jewish attitudes toward sexuality have been ambiguous for millennia, oscillating between mistrust and affirmation. We should be learning, she says, "to undercut dualisms, to find a way through and beyond the either/or thinking (either spirit or body, either virgin or whore) so central to western attitudes toward sexuality." [11] Bearing in mind that the body-versus-spirit division foundational to religion and philosophy in the western world is the same division that subordinates women to men, I think it is as important to question purely "secular" readings of the Song as it is to question purely "spiritual" ones. It is interesting that just as the age of science was dawning, a few critics in the seventeenth century began to read the Song as a secular epithalamion; that a view of it as secular love poetry became more frequent in the eighteenth century; and that this has become "the prevailing view." [12] A number of women writers have gone on record insisting that the Song should not be understood religiously at all. But in the Song that opposition is nonexistent.

Interpreters who claim that the Song is purely spiritual and not secular, and those who claim it is purely secular and not spiritual, are like the investigators of the elephant who think it is either only a trunk or only a tail. It makes so much more sense to say, with the commentator Roland Murphy, that the poem expresses "the recognition that human love and divine love mirror each other. . . . What links the literal sense of the Song to the expository visions of synagogue and church is an exquisite insight: the love that forms human partnership and community, and that sustains the whole of creation, is a gift of God's own self." [13] As the poet Grace Schulman also remarks, "it seems a pity to miss the Song's wider implications by regarding it as being either religious or secular, without entertaining simultaneously sacred and erotic interpretations. . . . Many deeply religious works are to be read with the whole of our sensibility, including physical love, and great love poems call for a spiritual reading as well." [14]

I think of the great thirteenth-century Persian poet Rumi, in one of his many poems addressed to a "you" he sometimes calls the Friend, who may be God, or a lover, or an aspect of the self: "I asked for one kiss. You gave me six" (1193), or "I thought I knew who I was,/ but I was you" (1242), or

> I've heard it said there's a window that opens
> from one mind to another,
> but if there's no wall, there's no need
> for fitting the window, or the latch. (511)

I think of the Hindu poet Mirabai singing to "the dark one," Krishna, "As the lotus lives in the water, I live in you." I think that when Nelly Sachs begins a poem by saying "perhaps God needs the longing," and goes on to declare, "O my beloved, perhaps in the sky of our longing worlds have been born of our love," she may be addressing a human lover, or a divine one, or both. And I think of myself as a girl, discovering in the long moments of kissing, embracing, touching the beautiful face and body of a boy, something I could only call holiness.

This is not a theoretical question. As the twentieth century closes and the twenty-first opens, as more women on the planet come to assume the sexual freedom of the Shulamite, sexuality has become a cause, a pretext, for global violence. The apparent issue is whether or not women are to be permitted to control their own bodies: do they belong to themselves or to their fathers, brothers, and husbands. We know what most "religions" think, yesterday and today. On this question the response of the Song of Songs is clear. The Shulamite is a free woman. The larger issue is the question of whether or not the human body is intrinsically shameful and evil. Again, this is a position commonly maintained by conventional "religious" thought. Increasingly in the West, however, there is a blossoming of an older and lovelier idea, the idea that the body is sacred. This idea animates the Song of Songs. Among Christian as well as Jewish theologians, the times are seeing a shift toward honoring the body and bodily love. Body and spirit are indivisible, for example, in John Carr's recent study of *The Erotic Word: Sexuality, Spirituality, and the Bible.*[15] In his discussion of the Song, Carr sees the lovers as melding with the natural world and translucent to the divine. This makes sense. We can almost imagine the sweetness and wholeness of it. Ultimately, a culture in which the deity's declaration "I will be your God, and you shall be my people" (Leviticus 26.12) parallels a bridegroom's wedding vow, and in which people are asked to love God with all their hearts, souls, and minds, can open itself to the twining of flesh and spirit in the Song of Songs. Yet it is difficult, as I will try to show later, to turn this dream or paradigm into real life.

Countertext: Content and Form

The Song is radical not only in its depiction of the physical fused with the spiritual. It imagines love without rules, it draws a positive picture of an assertive woman, it does not distinguish very strongly between men and women or between humanity and nature. In sum, it provides a picture of how the candle of love transforms whatever is seen in its light. This is what makes the Song of Songs a counter-text and defines its relation to the rest of the Bible.

All current biblical scholarship assumes that the Hebrew Bible is a set of widely various documents composed over a period of centuries if not millennia and redacted for several centuries more. Although fundamentalists and literalists continue to treat scripture as a monolithic book with a single message, contemporary commentary on the Bible emphasizes its heterogeneity and probes its fractures. Harold Bloom points out in *The Book of J* that the narrative voice in much of Genesis is far from pious. Anson Layton's *Arguing With God* examines the many biblical passages from Genesis to Job that either challenge or reject the assumption of God's goodness. Numerous feminist scholars, from Phyllis Trible in *God and the Rhetoric of Sexuality* to Ilana Pardes in *Countertraditions in the Bible,* while deploring biblical androcentrism and misogyny, discuss woman-centered passages in the Bible ranging in length from a phrase to a book. Biblical literature, according to these and many other accounts, is woven of surprisingly diverse sorts of yarn.

All such studies are explorations of counter-texts, a term I take from Pardes and employ to denote any biblical text, brief or extended, which in some fashion resists dominant structures of authority, divine and legal, as defined by the Bible as a whole and by the history of its interpretation. Major instances of counter-texts include antidoctrinal books like Job and Ecclesiastes, and woman-centered books like Ruth, Esther, and the Song of Songs. All the Writings, in fact, stand at diverse odd angles to the Law and the Prophets. But counter-texts also include brief episodes such as Abraham's bargaining with God at Mamre (Genesis 18), Rebecca's and Rachel's roles as tricksters (Genesis 27, 31), the wrestling of Jacob (Genesis 32), Tamar's gamble (Genesis 38), the midwives' civil disobedience (Exodus 1) and the conspiracy of women following it (Exodus 2), Moses' exclamation "Would that all the Lord's people were prophets!" (Numbers 11.29), Jeremiah's question of questions, "Why do sinners' ways prosper?" (Jeremiah 12.1), and the God of Isaiah (45.7) who asserts, "I form the light and create darkness; I make peace and create evil; I the Lord do all these things."

In one sense, then, the apparent anomaly of the Song of Songs is not anomalous at all. Still, by any measure, the Song constitutes the most remarkable countertext in an otherwise firmly patriarchal Hebrew canon. Whether we interpret it as a residue of prepatriarchal poetry inserted into the patriarchal context, or whether we see it as a later formation, the Song is, in effect, quintessentially nonpatriarchal. It mentions neither God nor any other superior being; it mentions neither law, ritual, the nation of Israel, the history of its people, nor the genealogies of its men. The Song features none of those "begats" that meant so much in the ancient world and mean so little to us now. It includes no representation of hierarchy or rule, no relationship of dominance and submission, and (almost) no violence. Whereas the Hebrew Bible concerns itself overwhelmingly with obedience and the New Testament responds by concerning itself with repentance and salvation, the Song inscribes an alternative story of voluntary love and pleasure.

Unlike the bulk of biblical narrative, which begins by granting mankind sovereignty over nature and pays little attention to the environment in which humans act thereafter (except to deal with issues of ownership), the Song is abundantly and tenderly descriptive. Its primary setting is a pastoral world of fertile nature, of flocks and birds, fruit trees and vineyards, gardens and oases, mountains and their wild creatures. The lovers are not "sovereign" over their environment, but virtually interchangeable with it. As he plans to adorn her with gold pendants and silver spangles, the young man compares his love to "a company of horses [Bloch translation *my mare,* with the understanding that mares inflame stallions] in Pharaoh's chariots." She replies as if he were a king sitting at table and then switches the venue, "A bundle of myrrh is my well-beloved unto me; he shall lie all night between my breasts" (1.9–14). "I am the rose of Sharon, the lily of the valleys," says the woman (2.1), and a little later,

> My beloved is mine and I am his; he feedeth among the lilies. Until the day break and the shadows flee away, turn, my beloved, and be thou like a roe or a young hart upon the mountains of Bether [alternate translation: mountains of spices]. (2.16–17)

To her, in one of his long speeches, he says,

> A garden inclosed is my sister, my spouse; a spring shut up, a fountain sealed. Thy plants are an orchard of pomegranates, with pleasant fruits; camphire, with spikenard, spikenard and saffron; calamus and cinnamon, with all trees of frankincense; myrrh and aloes, with all the chief spices. (4.12–14)

She then calls upon the north and south winds to blow upon her garden that the spices may flow out, and she urges, "Let my beloved come into his garden and eat his pleasant fruits" (4.16). All the lines that compare the beloved with some animal, as well as the refrain that asks the daughters of Jerusalem to swear by gazelles or does, imply acceptance and reverence for men's and women's own "animal" nature.

Descriptions like these alternate with the sumptuous setting of a noble or royal court, valued for its beauty rather than its political power. Place names in the Song are associated not with politics, war and conquest, but with pleasure and fantasy: the rose of Sharon, the cedars of Lebanon, the flock of goats from Mt. Gilead, the fishpools of Heshbon, and so on, are part and parcel of the lovers' play.

Rooted in wedding-songs or not, the Song depicts the joys of love unconnected with marriage or procreation. This is in sharp contrast to the normative models of sexuality in the Bible, in which women are property and wives are essentially breeders. Here the lovers mutually seek, mutually praise, mutually enjoy one another. For both, love is eating and drinking; kisses and embraces are like wine, the lover is a "tree whose fruit was sweet to my taste"; the woman is a garden in which the lover browses, eating the honeycomb with the honey. Both lovers are associated with doves, deer, gazelles. At times they mirror and echo each other's phrases, their speeches gliding into each other without the obstruction of "he said" and "she said":

> Let my lover come into his garden and eat his pleasant
> fruits. I am come into my garden, my sister, my spouse:
> I have gathered my myrrh with my spice. (4.16–5.1)

The drama of the poem rests not on any story of inaccessibility but on the fluctuations of presence and absence, pleasure anticipated and recollected, pleasure in the moment.[16]

Where the curse of Eve in Genesis declares that a woman's desire shall be for her husband and he shall rule over her, the woman in the Song proudly announces, "I am my beloved's, and his desire is for me" (7.10), a clear reversal of the curse. The woman speaks more lines of the dialogue, including the opening and the closing. She is also more aggressive, more introspective, and more philosophical than her lover. Hers is the quest for the beloved in the city streets, hers the adjuration to the daughters of Jerusalem not to awaken love until it is ripe, hers the fantasy that her lover might be like her brother, suckling from the same mother's breasts, hers the pronouncement that love is fierce as death and that the attempt to purchase it should be despised. Elsewhere in the Bible we are admonished to fear God. But in this text it is the woman who is awe inspiring, even terrifying, her eye glance dazzling to the lover, her presence "terrible as an army with banners" in the King James and Jewish Publication Society versions (cosmic as sun, moon, and stars in their courses, according to Ariel and Chana Bloch's translation of this obscure passage). Again, where Israelite social structure in the Bible is represented almost exclusively by men—the Book of Ruth is a partial exception—the Song does not mention fathers or the father's house, but twice mentions the mother's house as a place to bring the lover, even going so far as to suggest that the mother would instruct the daughter in the arts of lovemaking (8.2–3). It also provides a chorus of women, the daughters of Jerusalem, who speak antiphonally with the Shulamite in 5.8–10ff. and 6.1–2, in a way that suggests young women socializing independent of male control.

Two brief moments imply possible limits to the woman's freedom of erotic choice. In 1.6 she elliptically recalls her brothers' anger: "My mother's children were angry with me; they made me the keeper of the vineyards; But mine own vineyard have I not kept" (1.6). The tone might be equally regretful and apologetic, or mocking and defiant. In 5.8, when she seeks her lover through the nocturnal city streets—we do not know if this episode is a dream or a "real" event—the watchmen find her and beat her. A verse later, she seems unharmed as she engages in boastful dialogue with the daughters of Jerusalem over the beauties of her lover. Nothing in the Song suggests that woman is the second sex, in sharp distinction to her role everywhere else in scripture. Yet one does not, in reading the Song, think of the female as dominant over the male, thanks to the aura of pleasure enveloping both.

As unique as its content is the poem's form. Technically, the Song is designed in numerous ways to defy our normal sense of divisions and categories. The Masoretic version from which all our translations come takes the form of prose, cadenced but without line divisions, and part of the Song's erotic charm consists precisely in its dreamlike blurring of distinctions, as the speech of one lover glides into and is mirrored by the other's, and as one episode slips into the next without apparent boundaries. Numerous commentators have mentioned that it is sometimes difficult to tell who is speaking. The line between sleeping, waking, and fantasy experience is also at times unclear, as is the line between past, present, and future. In contrast to one of the dominant modes of biblical discourse—linear narrative of past events—the lyrics of the Song seem to unfold in a continuing present, with the reassuring occurrence of refrains, but no particular order.

Despite the efforts of generations of commentators to impose a "plot" on the Song, it goes nowhere and ends without closure. Ambiguity and riddling are part of its fabric. What is the meaning of the pronoun-slide in the poem's opening line? Is the Shulamite at first teasing her lover by speaking of him as "him" and then addressing him directly—perhaps after being kissed? Is she perhaps addressing her friends and then turning to him? Or is she perhaps speaking at first to herself and then to him? When we read the piquant "Let him kiss me with the kisses of his mouth, for your love is better than wine," all of these are real possibilities, and the blur of possibilities, unfortunately eliminated by many modern translations, is part of the essence of the Song. Millennia later, an equally ardent and riddling poet, Emily Dickinson, begins a poem that virtually defines the pleasures of poetry, by saying "I dwell in possibility——/ A fairer house than Prose."

Does the Shulamite say she is "black *but* comely" or "black *and* comely" (1.5)? The Hebrew *ve-* makes possible a deliciously ambiguous tone. Possibly she is defensive, if racial difference or agricultural work has darkened her skin, but possibly she is boasting. Are the lovers courtiers playing shepherds, or shepherds playing courtiers? In the spring song of 2.14–15, "Take us the foxes, the little foxes, that spoil the vines; for our vines have tender grapes," who are the "foxes"? Are they literal, or are they amorous young men and women as in an Ode of Theocritus? [17] In the passage of 8.8–10, just before it closes, an entirely new theme enters the poem:

> We have a little sister, and she hath no breasts; what shall we do for our sister in the day when she shall be spoken for? If she be a wall, we will build upon her a palace of silver; and if she be a door, we will inclose her with boards of cedar. I am a wall and my breasts are like towers; then was I in his eyes as one that found favour.

Who is the "little sister," not mentioned until this moment? Who is "we," and whose "eyes" are judging? [18] "One might be tempted to call the Song subversive, were it not the least polemical of books," remark the Blochs. Perhaps, though, the very absence of polemics makes it most deeply subversive because most deeply defiant of institutional religion's need to impose fixed order, meaning, and definition upon experience, to subdue reality to categories. In this respect it differs radically from Ecclesiastes and Job, those other extraordinary texts.

Among its many literary qualities, the most pervasively counter-textual is the Song's cascade of metaphors. For metaphoric language is the opposite of legal language, and legal pronouncement, along with narrative, is a dominant mode of biblical discourse, upon which much of what we take to be "Jewish" rests. Where the Law concentrates on establishing and maintaining distinctions—Israel versus the nations, man versus woman, clean versus unclean—metaphor requires that we apprehend likeness and difference simultaneously. Law strives for maximum precision; metaphor pulls away from precision and toward fluidity. Eluding fixity, metaphor produces not definitions but indefinite ripples of meaning. Due to the extraordinarily rich layering of metaphor in the Songs, we are prevented from thinking of humanity as dominant over animals and plants, or the beauties of artifact and architecture as altogether distinct from those of taste and smell, or eating and drinking as distinguishable from sex. As Robert Alter has astutely noted, "in the poetics of intertwinement manifested in the imagery of the poem, these seemingly opposed semantic fields actually overlap, run into each other." [19] At structural and linguistic levels, then, the Song replicates the absence of dominance and hierarchy, the blurring of boundaries and distinctions, which we see in the relationship of the lovers. As a secular text these characteristics render it exceptional enough. For those who experience the Song as erasing the border between sacred and secular, it offers a sense of the "holy" at odds with what is usually understood as "religious."

What then are the spiritual implications of the Song's portrait of mutual desire and joy? What happens when, having read the "simple" sense in some such way as I have done here, we consider what that sense signifies for our relationship with God? Despite certain readers who have asserted that desire is always *deferred* in the Song of Songs, I think of it as having been always already *satisfied* and hence anticipated with confidence rather than anxiety. Theologically, this would be equivalent to the conviction, the knowledge, that we are loved with an absolute love, by a being who has been present to us and will be present again. The happiness of the Song of Songs helps us, or can help us, to feel, to know, that this is indeed the case, and that that same love is extended to the world of which we are a portion. Again, where some readers assert that the erotic/spiritual experience toward which the Song gestures has something to do with "sovereignty," "mastery," "authority," one being subduing another—which is indeed what we find in most "religious" texts in the Western world—I conclude that the power relationships which dominate both religion and sex in our world (with each system of dominance reinforcing the other) have tragically blinded such readers even to the possibility of an alternative.[20] What is extraordinary in the Song is precisely the absence of structural and systemic hierarchy, sovereignty, authority, control, superiority, submission, in the relation of the lovers and in their relation to nature. The same holds for the relation of classes, since the shepherd may play the part of a king as well as the reverse, just as humans played the part of gods in celebrating sacred marriages in the pagan rituals from which these songs may be derived.

It seems to me that the relationship depicted in the Song of Songs, like every personal experience I have ever had of holiness, is defined by a sense of powerful connection, which is not subordination. I do not submit to the other; neither does the other submit to me. Light passes through us, and we see the light welling up in the world. This is quintessentially true of my relation with any beloved, any friend, when the connection feels blessed. Feels heavenly. I know, in those moments, that a spiritual world exists and that I belong to it. Not that this state of awareness is normal. But am I wrong to name it as my ideal desire? And am I wrong to fantasize, to dream, to imagine, to suppose, that God's love of us, and ours of God, might ideally be as ardent and as free of power-play as the love enacted in this Song? Progressive theology today asks us to "re-imagine the unimaginable" (Plaskow, ch. 4): to learn to see God not merely as the God-He who is father, warrior, judge, and not merely as disembodied *ein-sof*, but as the God-She of the mystics who is Shekhinah, wisdom, the God who is friend, companion, cocreator, the God who is both place and abyss, transcendant and immanent. Surely God is all these things; "diverse images of God are not the names of multiple divinities but guises of the One that manifests itself in and through the changing forms of the many."[21] And what of God as lover? The Song stares us in the face—unique among texts, a Holy of Holies. If we are to take the Song in its spiritual sense, then does it not invite us to affirm this wildest dream?

The Song and the Real World

What I have just written will seem absurd, I assume, to most readers. It seems absurd to me as well. God as lover? God as the lover who is equal to the self? God as the lover who takes no interest in control or dominance, but only in delight? Our spiritual quest as one in which God wants to meet us half-way? God's desire for us outside the Law? Impossible. And very much more impossible if we are women.[22]

Curiously enough, the Song itself offers a description and analysis of that seeming impossibility. When I teach the Song of Songs and describe it as differing from the dominant depictions of gender relations in the Bible—when I point out how Edenlike its world is, how nonoppressive, how nonviolent, and especially when I express my pleasure in the freedom of the Shulamite—students sometimes correct me by pointing to 5.2–8. In this passage the woman leaves her house to seek her beloved in the street. He has come nocturnally knocking at her door, saying "open to me, my sister, my love, my dove," but she hesitates, and by the time she opens to her beloved he is gone:

> I rose up to open to my beloved, and my hands dropped with myrrh, and my fingers with sweet smelling myrrh, upon the handles of the lock. I opened to my beloved; but my beloved had withdrawn himself, and was gone: my soul failed when he spake; I sought him, but I could not find him; I called him, but he gave me no answer. The watchmen that went about the city found me, they smote me, they wounded me; the keepers of the walls took away my veil from me.

What about *that,* my students ask indignantly. The minute the woman doesn't know her place, the minute she dares to go public, she gets beaten up and treated like a whore. By the cops. They probably rape her. They probably say she was asking for it.

When I reply that this scene is just a minor episode, a brief evocation of loss and pain that is quickly over and seems to be in the poem almost for the sake of contrast, to heighten our sense of the pleasure and safety that otherwise abound, these students shake their heads. They're not having any. They know better. For them, this scene and this scene alone is a portrait of the real world. In a sense, I have come to admit, they are right. Within the larger structure of the Bible, the Song is like a loophole through which we peek into an alternative existence. Within the Song, this episode is like a loophole through which we peer back at existence as we know it.

As has often been observed, it is impossible to ascertain whether 5.2–8 is a "real" event or a dream. Perhaps it is in

some sense both. "History is a nightmare from which I am
trying to awake," remarks Stephen Dedalus in *Ulysses;* and perhaps the exclusion of women from central spiritual roles in our
history should also be seen as a bad dream. A dream of several
thousand years. "Open to me," says the lover, but women un-
derstandably hesitate to do so. "I have put off my coat; how
shall I put it on? I have washed my feet; how shall I defile
them?" Better to stay safely in one's place, not make waves. For
what happens—according to respected Jewish tradition—to a
woman who goes public with her spiritual need, whose yearning is larger than a kitchen, who does not hide behind a *me-
hitza*? What happens to the learned Beruria, the only woman
whose opinions are cited in Talmud? Her devoted husband
Rabbi Meir instigates one of his disciples to seduce her in order to prove that women are flighty. When the disciple finally
overcomes her resistance, she kills herself for shame, but nobody seems to think Rabbi Meir should be ashamed. What
happens to Isaac Bashevis Singer's Yentl? It is impossible for
her to be both a woman and a scholar. What happens to the
women at the Wall? We are not speaking of allegory here, but
real life. Women who dare to pray aloud with Torah in hand at
the Kotel, the Western Wall in Jerusalem, have been spat on,
cursed, called whore. They have had chairs thrown at them,
they have been beaten up and hospitalized, and they—they,
not their assailants—have been arrested. Although nothing in
halakha, Jewish law, actually forbids these women's activity,
the Supreme Court of Israel pronounces that "custom" should
be observed. As of this date, women are permitted to gather as
a group at the Kotel but not to pray aloud, or carry Torahs, or
wear *tfillim* or prayer shawls. As it is uncannily written, "The
keepers of the walls took away my veil from me."

  For Christian women, the history is somewhat different. We know today that women were among the disciples of

Jesus and were active in the formation of the early Church and that women like the twelfth-century Hildegard of Bingen, the fourteenth-century Julian of Norwich and the sixteenth-century Teresa of Avila were powerful public figures as well as mystics in their own time. Yet we also know that Tertullian's view of women as "the devil's gateway" dominated Christianity for centuries. The Beguine poet and mystic Margerite Porete, burned at the stake in 1310, and Anne Hutchinson, excommunicated and banished from Massachusetts in 1637 for preaching, are but two instances of the danger faced by women who claim independent spiritual vision. Joan of Arc became a saint, but first she was burnt. Many, if not all, Christians today cling to the view that a man should be the woman's head just as Christ is the man's head, while women should "learn in silence with all subjection. . . . I suffer not a woman to teach, nor to usurp authority over the man, but to be in silence" (I Timothy 2.11–12).

Today, when women everywhere in the world are less and less willing to be silent, it becomes possible to dream of a time when women's spiritual insights, experiences, revelations, and passions will contribute as much as men's have done throughout history. As that time approaches, the meanings we give to God and the soul, to truth and goodness, to reality itself, will inevitably change. Perhaps our longing for a divinity we can love without fear will come closer to being answered.

The text of Song of Songs 5.8 requires particular attention, for it places the Shulamite in a social context. The King James version reads, "I charge you, O daughters of Jerusalem, if ye find my beloved, that ye tell him, that I am sick of love." In the Jewish Publication Society version, "I adjure you, O daughters of Jerusalem, If ye find my beloved, what will ye tell him? that I am love-sick." The Bloch version has "Swear to me, daughters of Jerusalem!" Exum has "I place you

under oath, women of Jerusalem." What is interesting here
is the legal language, earlier used apparently playfully—I
charge you, or adjure you, or ask you to swear, that you won't
waken love until it is ready—and here in earnest. Or perhaps
both usages are more earnest than we imagine. In a society
where marriages are arranged by the parents of the bride
and groom, it is revolutionary to argue for love-marriage. In
a society whose Law divides a woman's prayer from a man's
prayer, which forbids women to testify in a court of law, in
which, to use Rachel Adler's phrase, a woman is "the Jew who
wasn't there,"—what is perpetuated is injustice.[23] When the
Shulamite appeals to the daughters of Jerusalem with the so-
lemnity of an oath, she should awaken our longing for justice:
"Justice, justice shalt thou seek." When she cries that she is
sick with love—sick because of frustrated love—she should
remind us of our own condition. She begs us to be her allies.
We ought to answer her call.

But in the first place, we ought to respond to the call of
the Holy One. *Kol dodi! Kol dodi dofek!* The voice of my beloved. My beloved knocking. *Pitkhi li!* Open to me, says the
lover. And why? Though the language is somewhat obscure,
the translations converge on something like "For my head is
filled with dew, my locks with the drops of the night." Which
is to say that the Holy One, *baruch ha-shem,* our lover, is out
there in night and fog. The night and fog that might be not
only World War II (could Resnais have possibly been thinking of this image in the Song as an image for the incompre-
hensibility of the holocaust?) but all of human history. The
night and fog (and it ought to break our hearts to think this)
is all of Jewish history, too.

Kol dodi. In night and fog—from who knows how far
back, from the time of the Kingdom, from the time of exile, the time of Akiva, throughout the diaspora to this very

moment—the lover knocks at our womanly door, saying
Open to me. And we want to open, but we're afraid, and when
we go to the door it's too late, and we regret our hesitation:
Nafshi yatzeah ve-dabbero, my soul failed at his speech. But
the Song is timeless, the Song is still there, the beloved still
knocks. How long will it take us to answer fearlessly?

THE BOOK OF RUTH AND
THE LOVE OF THE LAND

The earth is the Lord's, and the fulness thereof,
the world, and those who dwell therein.

— PSALM 23

T o state the obvious: women have been noticing for at least a century and a half that the Bible is dominated by males and masculinity.[1] Its God is supposedly sexless, but the pronouns for God are masculine, the roles of God are almost all male—father, king, warrior, judge—and glorify male power and authority. The human beings chosen to enact God's will in history are, with very few exceptions, men: patriarchs, warriors, judges, kings, priests, prophets. Beginning with the tenth commandment, which declares, "You shall not covet your neighbor's wife, nor his male servant, nor his female servant, nor his ox, nor his ass, nor anything that is your neighbor's" (Exodus 20.17), Hebrew law addresses itself to a community of men for whom women are articles of property. To read the narratives as history, beginning with Genesis and going forward through the Exodus stories into the annals of monarchy, is to watch, as if in slow motion, the gradual formation of a nation-state in which women as active members of a pastoral and nomadic society virtually disappear under the dominating shadow of priestly, military, and monarchic principles.

Yet when we look between the cracks of this great found-
ing scripture designed to support a social hierarchy whose
wives and daughters will be subordinate to husbands and fathers, we can find tracks and traces of women's truths, wom-
en's values, women's powers. The Book of Ruth is a prime
instance. Like the Song of Songs, Ruth is a counter-text that
reimagines the roles of men and women, but it does more than
that. For where the Song is about the ravishment of young
love, Ruth is about the choices and meanings of maturity, including what I would call political maturity. To read Ruth
with attention and enjoyment is to experience an interlocking
array of ways in which this story radically deviates from biblical norms while yet remaining seamlessly attached to them.
This seamlessness is an important fact for traditionalists as
well as feminists to recognize. Ruth demonstrates that we can
imagine a more egalitarian future, while remaining inspired
by our sources in the past. Confronted with a polarized choice
of "either/or," we can respond "both/and." So, I want to make
clear, the Book of Ruth departs from biblical norms in four
crucial ways, yet it never breaks away from its biblical context
into protest or polemic, but integrates a radical vision into an
ongoing tradition.[2]

Here are the departures that interest me: First, the genre
of Ruth is essentially pastoral, though woven into history. It
is an idyll, taking place during a lovely loophole of peace between wars, a fact that is crucial to its other deviant qualities. Second, it is women-centered whereas most of the Bible
centers on male figures, though its closure returns to a male
story. The women in the Book of Ruth take chances, calcu-
late, assert themselves, and succeed. Third, God's presence in
the Book of Ruth is uniquely tied up with fertility and is represented chiefly through invocation, as if God were made real
through human discourse, through the fertility of the heart.

Finally, the book's view of land and of boundaries between lands is also unique, not duplicated anywhere else in the Bible, yet tied to biblical themes of land use and inheritance. And I want to suggest that these differences are interdependent.

Gender and Genre

Briefly to recapitulate the story: the Book of Ruth begins with a famine in the city of Bethlehem in Judah from which a man named Elimelech flees to the neighboring country of Moab with his wife Naomi and two sons. Elimelech dies; the sons marry Moabite women and live there for ten years; then they too die. The bitter Naomi, learning of a good crop in Bethlehem, decides to return and vehemently urges her daughters-in-law to return to their own mothers' houses and find themselves new husbands. Orpah agrees, but Ruth, clinging to her mother-in-law, utters one of the most poignant speeches in scripture: "Entreat me not to leave you," she says to Naomi. "For wherever you go, I will go. Wherever you lodge I will lodge. Your people shall be my people and your God my God. Where you die I will die and there I will be buried. May the Lord do so to me and more if anything but death parts me from you" (1.16). Or, in another possible translation, "if even death parts us." [3]

When Naomi sees how determined Ruth is to go with her, she ceases to argue and the two go on until they reach Bethlehem. Here they are greeted by a chorus of women who are amazed to see Naomi again. Angrily, she tells them not to call her "Naomi" (sweetness) but "Mara" (bitterness) because the Lord has dealt bitterly with her: she went out full, and God has returned her empty. As readers, we may at this point notice that Naomi makes no reference to Ruth. Soon,

however, as it is barley harvest time, Ruth goes out to glean
in the fields after the reapers have been through. To glean
is to gather by hand what harvesters have left behind, and
in Jewish law gleaning is a privilege of the poor. Here Ruth
encounters the landowner, Boaz, and we have a second crucial dialogue. Boaz calls her "my daughter" and bids her glean
freely in his fields; he tells his reapers to leave extra gleanings
for her and instructs the men not to molest her. She bows to
the ground before him and asks why he is so kind to her, a
foreigner; he replies that he has heard of her kindness to her
mother-in-law and how she left her own country for a land
she did not know. He ends his speech with a blessing, "May
the Lord reward your deeds. May you have a full recompense
from the Lord God of Israel, under whose wings [or "skirt" or
"robe"] you have sought refuge." She in turn thanks him for
comforting her even though she is not one of his maidservants,
and hopes she will find favor in his sight. He then gives
her food and urges her to eat among his workers (2.8–14).
When Ruth recounts her story in the evening, Naomi praises
God and announces that Boaz is a kinsman of Elimelech—
"goel, a redeeming kinsman," which in Jewish law meant
that he was legally entitled to redeem property belonging to
Elimelech.

So the plot thickens, and soon it thickens further. When
the barley harvest and wheat harvest are done, Naomi instructs Ruth in a bold plan: she is to dress up and perfume
herself, go to the threshing floor at night, find where Boaz
is sleeping after the harvest festivities, uncover his feet and
lie down next to him. As the original audience for the tale
would have known, "feet" in ancient Hebrew was often
a euphemism for another part of a man. Ruth does what
Naomi suggests—and when Boaz wakes, startled, we have a
third dialogue: "Who are you?" "I am your handmaid Ruth.

Spread your robe (or wings) over your handmaid, for you are a *goel*." "Be blessed of the Lord, daughter," he replies. "Your latest deed of loyalty [or loving kindness] is greater than the first, for you have not turned to younger men whether poor or rich" (3.9–10).

In the final chapter of the book of Ruth we have first some negotiations: Boaz gives a nearer kinsman the opportunity to redeem a parcel of land belonging to Elimelech and to marry Ruth; when this man refuses (thus paralleling Orpah), Boaz takes Ruth as his wife with the blessing of the town's elders. Ruth bears a son, and the women congratulate Naomi: "Blessed be the Lord, who has not withheld a redeemer from you. . . . He will renew your life and sustain your old age, for he is born of your daughter-in-law Ruth, who loves you and is better to you than seven sons" (4.15). In a coda to the story, a genealogy tells us that this son, Obed, becomes the father of Jesse and the grandfather of King David.

Generations of readers have enjoyed the unique qualities of the Book of Ruth, which so clearly has elements of folktale, and yet is composed with exquisite art, like a cantata in which every note counts and resonates, along with a finely balanced structure, eloquent and elegant dialogue, and a fullness of wordplay and allusion which deepens and transforms its meaning. Though we know nothing of its origin, Ruth is among the few portions of the Bible that may originate in women's storytelling traditions.[4] At the same time the book is evidently intended to provide an ancestry for David and consequently of the Messiah, who is also to come from the root of Jesse.[5] Some scholars have speculated that it is a Hebraized adaptation of the Eleusinian mysteries around Demeter and Persephone or a historicized version of the epic of the Canaanite goddess Anat. Yet it is read at the time of the feast of

Shavuoth, which celebrates the giving of the Torah at Sinai and sealing the covenant between God and the children of Israel. In other words, women's and men's traditions have been blended to form this book.

The opening phrase of Ruth tells us that the story takes place "in the days when the judges ruled," and the contrast between the Book of Judges and the Book of Ruth is overwhelming. Judges is a book of relentless violence, slaughter, and war, both external and internal. It also contains the horrific stories of Jephthah's daughter and the Levite's concubine and perfectly illustrates the fact that a militarized society is a bad thing for women. This is the case even though Judges also contains the tales of competently aggressive women, Deborah, Yael, and Delilah. If the text of Judges is warfare, then its subtext is gender war. Nowhere in Judges do we see a shred of kindness between any two people. Ruth, in tonic contrast, is a pastoral. It occurs in peacetime, its plot does not turn on conflict, its values have nothing to do with conquest and killing but with personal and family relationships, fertility and ongoing life. Although it begins with a famine precipitating the plot, its major scenes occur during a time of plentiful harvest, and the connection between natural harvest and human sexuality and fruitfulness is obvious. Like many pastorals, it uses sexually suggestive but not sexually explicit language and scenes; for example, it capitalizes on the ambiguity of Boaz's "feet" and on the suggestiveness of the threshing floor (a place of lascivious activity in Hosea 9.1), while maintaining an aura of innocence about its protagonists. The double entendres in the text may even include *kanaph*—that which Boaz is invited to cover Ruth with—variously interpreted as skirt, wing, robe, corner of a garment, or extremity. In Deuteronomy 27.20, *kanaph* is a euphemism for the father's genitals, so we may have an additional ticklish hint of provocative meaning when Boaz expresses the hope that Ruth will be protected by God's *kanaph*.

It is easy to imagine communal giggling around the fire when the storyteller gets to the place where Ruth lies down next to (or is it with?) Boaz all night and again when Boaz outwits the John Doe next-of-kin, and it is equally easy to imagine the sighs of satisfaction at the happy ending. The Book of Ruth is deeply optimistic, with an optimism generated not in the usual biblical way by concentrating on ideas of nationhood and obedience to law, but by looking at the possibilities of *chesed,* or loving kindness—lovingly generous human behavior at the most intimate of levels.

Then there is the gynocentric factor. As peace is required for the enactment of pastoral, peace also makes possible a story centered on two women. That the Book of Ruth is woman-centered is obvious, but just *how* woman-centered may not be so evident on the surface. As has often been noticed, Naomi and Ruth make their way alone and destitute in a world where women without male protection are utterly at risk, and they do so by a combination of mutual caring and initiative taking of a sort that does not occur elsewhere in the Bible. Ruth's abandonment of her own family and nation to cling to Naomi is unprecedented for a woman; her gleaning represents initiative and energy; and her dialogues with Boaz demonstrate something very close to manipulativeness. As my delighted students point out, she is definitely flirting.[6] At the same time, Naomi's shift from alienation to connection represents hope for a class of people, widows without sons, usually seen as without resource, the lowest of the low. The relationship between Naomi and Ruth is unique in a world where rivalry between women is the norm enforced by a social structure in which women are completely reliant on men for both life and self-esteem. Think of Sarah and Hagar, Rachel and Leah, Hannah and Peninah. No friendship, let alone love, is imagined between any of these co-wives. But in the Book of Ruth, as Phyllis Trible initially observed, "One female has chosen another female in a world where life depends upon men. There is no more radical decision in all the memories of Israel."[7] If in our own time Ruth's vow has become the model for wedding vows both heterosexual and same-sex, then we can see this as the radical afterlife of what is initially unique: love of one woman for another which is neither mandated nor disrupted by patriarchal law.[8]

But there is more. Ruth is the only book of the Bible besides the Song of Songs that gives us a hint of a women's community and social life existing alongside yet distinct from male society. When Naomi tells her daughters-in-law not to follow her, she tells them to return to their *mothers'* houses, not their fathers'. Later, the women who greet Naomi and at the tale's close congratulate her, offer blessing, and name the newborn child, are like a chorus around the main action. The daughters of Jerusalem, invoked by the Shulamite in the Song of Songs, form another such chorus, though less grounded in a sense of ongoing community life. The presence of this chorus, as well as the liveliness and the use of dialogue in the story, makes one wonder if it might originally have been a theatrical entertainment, perhaps something performed at harvest time in ancient Judah. But there is also more than this, and here it is important to look at the extraordinary allusiveness of the book of Ruth and what it signifies.

Is Naomi merely an individual widow with a good daughter-in-law who makes things turn out happily for her? Is Ruth merely an individual who forms an individual attachment to her mother-in-law which turns out happily? Not exactly. In rabbinic commentary, Ruth is the paradigmatic convert and Naomi the paradigmatic teacher of *halakha,* Jewish law, but we discover more surprising aspects of the two characters when we see them in the light of other biblical characters. For the verbal links of this story to other stories give it a depth far beyond the folktale aspect of loyalty rewarded, but also different from a classic conversion narrative. Naomi, complaining to Ruth and Orpah that "the hand of the Lord has gone forth against me" (1.13), and later to her former neighbors that "the Lord has testified against me, and Shaddai has afflicted me" (1.21), is a female version of Job. Job, too, uses legal metaphors and speaks "*bemar nafshi*"—in the bitterness of my spirit. Not only grieving but angry, Naomi like Job rejects proffered comfort and directly blames God for her woes. Moreover, one name she uses for God, *Shaddai,* typically translated "Almighty" in English, also appears several times in Job and comes from Hebrew and Akkadian words for breast or hill, so that the God being addressed might best be translated God of the breast-hill-mountain. It is a name often used in connection with the blessings of fertility. Thus, the underlying issue here is not merely one woman's bad luck but the benevolence or cruelty of God. Perhaps surreptitiously, the issue is also the gender of God.

And what of Ruth? As more than one commentator notes, Ruth is a female version of the patriarch Abraham, who in Genesis 12.1 is told by God to "go from your country and your kindred and your father's house to the land that I will show you." She too leaves family and country behind, in a leap of faith. As Boaz says admiringly to her (2.11), "you came to a people that you did not know before." And she goes not commanded by God, or even encouraged, but out of love. She is not "chosen"; she chooses. She herself chooses. She makes a covenant. In a sense she is something greater than Abraham; that is, if he represents a past in which humanity must be told what to do, she represents a future in which the heart itself judges rightly. At the same time we may note that Ruth's extraordinary clinging or cleaving to Naomi is like that of Adam to Eve, flesh of flesh, bone of bone, about which we are told that therefore a man will leave father and mother and cleave to his wife. It is also like the defiant love of Jonathan for David, in which a father's will and inheritance are rejected for the sake of a beloved. As Ruth declares her vows to Naomi, so Jonathan's soul knits with the soul of David (I Samuel 18.1). The male story is, of course, tragic, the women's story joyous.

But even these are not the only strands tying Ruth to other portions of the Bible. Boaz calls Ruth *eshet chayil,* woman of valor, and the listeners to the tale would recognize this familiar expression, a male version of which is used to introduce Boaz himself. It also appears in the Exodus story when Moses has to delegate authority to *anashim chayil,* men of valor. The term suggests leadership, worth, courage. The Ruth of this story is not Keats's Ruth, listening to the nightingale, sick for home, standing "in tears amid the alien corn." On the contrary, though she is certainly an alien, she is also a woman of expedition and action. We as audience recognize the accuracy of Boaz's epithet for her, for we see that Ruth always bravely goes further than she is told. In the scene at the threshing house, most dramatically, she has been told by Naomi to lie down next to Boaz and let him tell her what to do (3.4). Instead of this, while behaving with perfect demureness, it is she who tells him. When he wakes and asks "Who are you," and she answers, "I am Ruth, your handmaid; spread your robe [wings] over your handmaid, for you are a *goel*" (3.9), she performs several rather deft rhetorical moves. To start, she advances her position from maidservant (2.13) to handmaid, a term implying greater intimacy. She also reminds Boaz of his own earlier phrasing to her, in which he hoped that she would receive a full reward from "the Lord God of Israel, under whose wings [or robe] you have come to take refuge" (2.12), as it were pointing out to him that he has the capacity to bring this wish to fulfillment. Finally, she conflates his status as *goel,* a family member who can redeem a piece of land, with that of the brother of a deceased man who would be expected under levirate law to marry a widow.

We may notice thematic echoes of the daughters of Lot (Genesis 19) and of Tamar's seduction of Judah (Genesis 38) in this episode; like those earlier women, if more delicately, Ruth is taking the law into her own hands. Aviva Zornberg points out that what is usually translated as an imperative—spread your robe—is actually a simple future tense—you will spread your robe. And what Zornberg hears is a strange echo of what we hear in Exodus 20: "I am the Lord your God, and you will have no other gods. . . ." "I am Ruth your handmaid, and you will spread your robe. . . ." *Anochi adonai elohekha. . . . Anochi Ruth amatekha. . . .*[9] Like God, Ruth says things, and they come to pass. Trust, faith, confidence, and virtue bring them, as it were, to pass, as the story deftly weaves a web in which women are at the center, attached by verbal and thematic strands to some of the most important themes of the Bible: doubt and faith, exile and wandering, sexuality and love and progeny, God's power and human actions. The centrality of women transforms these themes, feminizing them in such a way as to make them nonviolent, producing a conflict-reduction story. At the same time, we are given a unique idea of how God enters the human world.

God and Man in Bethlehem

If Ruth is linked to God by her choice, Boaz is likened to God by his actions. He is a redeemer, he will spread his robe, he acts with *chesed,* kindness, to the living and the dead. This diffusion of godlike *chesed* brings us to another curious facet of the Book of Ruth: the role of God. In most biblical narratives, God is an active agent, very much on the scene, intervening with a vengeance. In the narratives of Judges, we see God repeatedly controlling the action, and when we are told that the spirit of God, *ruach adonai,* descends on someone, it means that the man has become an especially fierce warrior, as in the stories of Jephthah (Judges 11.29) and Samson (Judges 14.6, 14.19, 15.14). In Ruth, however, God takes note of his people and gives them food near the beginning of the story; at its close, the Lord gives conception to Ruth, and she bears a son. He is in effect if not in name, a fertility God rather than a war God. Between the opening and the close God does not appear but is continually invoked. "May the Lord deal kindly with you as you have dealt with the dead and with me," Naomi says to her daughters-in-law in 1.8. In 1.13 she is negative and accuses God of causing her suffering. Immediately afterward, Ruth in her great oath-taking speech declares allegiance to Naomi and to God, swearing fidelity unto death to Naomi, in God's name. Naomi again rails against God at her return to Bethlehem. So in this opening chapter there is a kind of oscillation about God: God is a source not only of benevolence but perhaps also of malevolence.

In the second chapter this shifts. Boaz appears in the field, and he and his workers exchange a gracious greeting and response: "The Lord be with you," he says to them, and they reply, "The Lord bless you" (2.4). With this we immediately feel Boaz's goodness and a sort of penumbra of God's goodness. This is heightened when he speaks to Ruth: he knows her kindness to Naomi and invokes God to reward her deeds. When Ruth tells Naomi what happened that first day in the field, Naomi exclaims, "Blessed be he by the Lord, whose *chesed*/kindness has not forsaken the living or the dead" (2.20).

Is the constant one God or Boaz? We cannot tell. When sur-
prised by Ruth, Boaz exclaims, "May you be blessed by the
Lord, my daughter" (3.10), and ends his speech by swearing in
God's name to find Ruth a redeemer or become that person
himself. When he publicly announces his intention to marry
Ruth, the elders and all the people at the city gate declare
their hope that the Lord will make her fruitful. When she
gives birth, the women bless the Lord one more time.

All this invoking of God's benevolence is reinforced by
the idea of redemption. The term signifies responsibility and
accountability; the *goel* is a kinsman willing to buy back lost
or forfeited property for its original owners, and there is obviously both a practical and a spiritual dimension to the term.
The root *gal* (redeem) occurs twenty-one times in the story,
always referring to human beings as redeemers, but no listener
would fail to connect the term with the familiar epithet for
God, *goel Yisrael,* the redeemer of Israel. It is also supported
by the repeated verb *davak,* cling or cleave: Ruth clings to
Naomi, Boaz tells her to cling to the girls in his fields, and the
echo comes not only from Adam and Eve, but also from Deuteronomy, where the verb is repeatedly used to describe devotion to God. The overwhelming effect in the Book of Ruth is
that God and human beings seem to mirror each other. God's
kindness, invoked by human beings, is also enacted by them.
To put it another way, the kindness of human beings reveals
the kindness of a God who "acts through human agents . . .
when people act with *chesed,* God is acting in them." [10]

The Poetry of the Land

The significance of land as the source of fertility is taken for
granted everywhere in the Bible. But here we have also to

consider another linked theme of the Book of Ruth: the idea that, as the twenty-fourth Psalm says, "The earth is the Lord's and the fulness thereof, the world, and those who dwell therein." For the Book of Ruth is an extraordinary illustration of a possible meaning of those words, a redeemed meaning, if I can put it that way, that acts as counterbalance or antidote to the usual biblical connection made between God's ownership of the world—of the land—and his power as "king of glory; the Lord strong and mighty, the Lord mighty in battle." For the Lord has nothing to do with military might in the present story. There are no battles. And here I turn to speak of the book's poetry and its deep ethical significance, if I can, as an amazing fusion.

When Ruth and Boaz marry, theirs is not just any happy marriage. Ruth is a Moabite, and for much of Biblical history the Hebrew people are commanded to treat Moab as an eternal enemy. "No Ammonite or Moabite shall enter the assembly of the Lord," commands Deuteronomy 23.3, both because this people stem from the incestuous union of Lot with his daughter and are therefore identified with licentiousness, and because they refused aid to the children of Israel during their sojourn in the wilderness. In Numbers 25, when "the people began to play the harlot with the daughters of Moab," an angered God sends a plague. Yet Ruth crosses the border between the land of Moab and the land of Judah and is accepted. Nothing in the text questions the legitimacy of her entry among the Israelite people or of her marriage to one of them, or treats these events as a problem. The rabbinic midrash does not overlook the problem, but ingeniously declares that a new law, promulgated in Boaz's time, prohibited "Ammonite but not Ammonitess, Moabite but not Moabitess." Of this, there is no trace in the story. Boaz, moreover, as a genealogy tells us, stems from the union of Tamar with Judah—a righteous union into which she tricked him by pretending to be a prostitute when he failed to honor the code of levirate marriage requiring a dead man's brother or other next of kin to marry his widow. The code Judah tried to elude is precisely the code Boaz feels called to obey. Ruth and Boaz, then, represent boundary-crossing, both geographical and moral. What is most marginal becomes the center. What is unacceptably transgressive becomes, in this story, welcome.

Now, what does *land* signify in this picture? Not that which is to be either conquered or defended. I want to suggest that it means *potential for life* and that *fertile land* mediates between God and human beings. There is a leitmotif running through the story, in transformative ripples, which in poetic terms creates a charming music and in ethical terms a morality based in generosity. I will try to suggest how this works, although it takes reading the whole book as if it were a poem to hear what I hope to get at and although the Hebrew meanings are in part effaced by translation.

First, in the opening sentence of the book of Ruth we encounter a sort of verbal paradox: famine in the *land (ha-eretz)* affects the city of Bethlehem—*Beit-lechem,* the *house of bread.* From there Elimelech goes to what most translations call the *country* of Moab but which is literally the *fields* of Moab. After the account of the deaths of Elimelech and his sons, the term is repeated twice, as Naomi decides to return from the *fields of Moab* because God has given his people *bread,* and she then sets forth for the *land of Judah.* So there is this chiastic opening movement of exile and return, of which the music is *land, bread, fields,* then *fields, bread, land.* The close of chapter 1 is a bit of recapitulation and the beginning of a linked leitmotif: "Thus Naomi returned from the *fields of Moab.* . . . they arrived in *the house of bread* at the beginning of the *barley harvest.*"

In chapter 2, this second leitmotif, the theme of harvest, moves forward. Chapter 2 continues to use the terms *fields* and *field,* though now we are looking at the field of Boaz, a verbal parallel to the fields of Moab. To this thread is joined active imagery of harvest: gleaning among the ears of grain, gleaning in a field behind the reapers, gleaning and gathering among the sheaves behind the reapers. Boaz tells Ruth not to glean in another field, but to keep her eyes on the field his girls are reaping; she gets up after lunch to glean, he gives orders to his reapers to let her glean—the terms are like a refrain all through here, and at the close of chapter 2 comes the refrain of fulfillment; Ruth quotes Boaz as saying "cling to my workers . . . until all my harvest is finished," and the narrator tells us she clings to Boaz's maidservants and gleans until the barley harvest and the wheat harvest were finished. The continued "clinging," usually translated "keep fast by" or "stay close to," continues the motif of erotic/devoted connection initiated in chapter 1.

We advance in chapter 3 from harvest to winnowing on the threshing floor, and this term too is repeated: "go down to the threshing floor," "so she went down to the threshing floor," "let it not be known that a woman came to the threshing floor." Alongside this imagery of separating grain from chaff, which supports the theme of natural fruitfulness but also the concept of life-altering decision making, together with the sexual overtones, we have the crucial terms *goel/gal,* redeemer/redeem, recurring five times, and the "six measures of barley" Boaz gives Ruth, repeated twice. Lastly, as we move into the final chapter of the Book of Ruth, variations on the term redeemer and redeem recur an astonishing twelve times in the first eight verses—along with the *field of Moab* from which Naomi has returned and the *field of Elimelech,* which she is selling. Here the verbal reprise is also a surprise in terms of plot. We have not been told of this field before—and almost the instant that we learn of it we learn also that whoever redeems this field must also acquire Ruth with it. Though the word is not used here, Ruth is in effect clinging to this field. Whoever takes the land, takes also the woman. When one man does not, the other does. At the book's close the term *redeemer* is suddenly used for the child born to Ruth and Boaz.

Why have we not heard earlier of this parcel of land? Why does it appear only in the tale's final chapter? One reason is, of course, that mentioning it earlier might spoil our sense of Naomi and Ruth's entire destitution. A more interesting reason is that the narrator is moving us more and more deeply as the story proceeds, into matters of Jewish law and ethics, including the issue of the treatment of strangers, the laws around gleaning, the law of levirate marriage, and culminating in the figure of redemption.

Ruth's acceptance by the Israelite community has been mandated by divine commandment, which insists that the stranger—the foreigner—be treated with fairness and even with love. "There shall be one law for the native and for the stranger who sojourns among you" (Exodus 12.49) is the opening utterance of a theme that appears again and again among God's orders to the children of Israel. Exodus 20.10 explicitly exempts the stranger from work on the sabbath. Exodus 22.21, declaring what was to be learned from oppression, "You shall not wrong a stranger or oppress him, for you were strangers in the land of Egypt," is later emphatically augmented in Leviticus 19.33, where "the stranger who sojourns with you shall be to you as the native among you, and you shall love him as yourself; for you were strangers in the land of Egypt: I am the Lord your God." When a commandment ends with this phrase it is as if God is saying: Pay attention to this one, I really mean it. In Deuteronomy 10.14–19, God's universalism spills over into a stirring plea for universal kindness, God's impartial love into a mandate for humans:

> Behold, to the Lord your God belong the heaven and the heaven of heavens, the earth, with all that is in it. Yet the Lord set his heart in love upon your fathers and chose their descendants [Heb. "seed"] after them. . . . Circumcise therefore the foreskin of your heart, and be no more stubborn [Heb. "stiffnecked"]. For the Lord your God is God of gods, and Lord of lords . . . who is not partial and takes no bribe. He executes justice for the fatherless and widow, and loves the stranger, giving him food and clothing. Love therefore the stranger: for you were strangers in the land of Egypt.

We may plausibly assume that such edicts were honored in the breach more than in the observance, just as they are today. They are not mentioned in the text, however, and are alluded to only in Ruth's first speech to Boaz in the field, where she identifies herself as a stranger. Boaz honors them, as it were, instinctively. Then, care for the stranger in Ruth coincides with commandments regarding land because the right of the poor and the stranger to glean is but one of numerous commandments insisting that the collectivity of Israel support those who are poor among them. "When you reap the harvest of your land, you shall not reap your field to the very border, neither shall you gather the gleanings after your harvest" (Leviticus 19.9) is repeated in Leviticus 23.22, which adds, "you shall leave them for the poor and the stranger; I am the Lord your God." Leviticus 25.23, referring to the law saying that land sold in bad times had to be returned to its original owner in the Jubilee year, makes clear that private property is never merely private: "The land must not be sold in perpetuity, for the land is mine; for you are strangers and sojourners with me."

When Boaz not only urges Ruth to continue working in his fields but also orders his men not to molest her and to leave extra ears of corn for her, and when he offers her food and drink, he is clearly obeying the letter of the law, and then some. Similarly, when he takes up Ruth's challenge to be both a *goel* and a husband, he is again doing more than the law requires. For he clearly has to engage in some manipulation of the nearer kinsman in order to act as redeemer of the field, and the law of levirate marriage, which Ruth seems to invoke, does not in fact apply to him since he is not a brother of the deceased husband.

Thinking about Boaz's combination of wealth and *menschlichkeit,* one thinks of King Lear's demand that the rich "shake the superflux" to the poor "and show the heavens more just." In Ruth as in Lear, we encounter—though less explicitly—the possibility that divine justice is demonstrated through the goodness of human beings, and not otherwise. What charms us in Ruth is the inextricability of ethical behavior from erotic gratification. Is Boaz doing the right thing, and more than the right thing, is he acting as God wishes men of honor to act because he is attracted to this attractive female? Well, yes. And is he attracted to her in part because she herself has behaved honorably, beyond the line of duty? Yes again. So eros and ethics join at the moment of harvest.

Now, what do these ripples of terms—*bread, land, fields, harvest, threshing, cling, redemption, field*—moving so musically through the text of the Book of Ruth, tell us about land? Several things. That land is in part collective, in part private property, but collective boundaries may be crossed in an act of loving kindness, fields on one side of an ethnic border are very like fields on the other side, and the borders of private land ideally are not purely private. Rather, private property in a world that follows God's dictates is the instrument of generosity; the deity who is the creator and real owner of the earth acts as both model and mandator for sharing its wealth. Property in this tale clings to responsibility; fruitfulness is connected to human fruitfulness. Instead of the sharp divisions we are accustomed to encountering in most of the Bible between God and man, male and female roles, one nation versus another nation, our own people and the Other—divisions which, we need scarcely note, govern most of human society today as well—the book of Ruth gives us a sense of blendings, clingings, continuum. Not either/or. Not this land versus that land. Land and fields are in themselves neutral, but can yield a harvest, harvest can be shared, sharing can itself yield a bountiful harvest: moreover, this imagery of fertility comes to fruition in the birth of a child, a son: *he* is a redeemer and will be the grandfather of the great redeemer King David. Ultimately, *land,* in this story, stands between God and human beings; land mediates generosity—not only sustaining life and creating new life, but making community possible, making links between communities possible, and linking problematic past to covenanted future.

To summarize: The Book of Ruth is an exquisite and transformative counter-text within the overwhelmingly patriarchal design of the Bible, linking several motifs, not least of which is the motif of land. Whereas the dominant narrative mode is epic, the Book of Ruth is pastoral and idyllic. It is erotic and woman-centered rather than heroic or legalistic. Or, to put it more radically, in Ruth, heroic impulses and legalistic precisions serve the cause of eros, making this book a counterweight and antidote to the war stories of the Book of Judges.[11] Stretching our notion of community and nation, Ruth quietly endorses the acceptance of the Other, the outsider. Here, for once, we learn how to make love not war, how to love and accept those who are conventionally supposed to be our enemies. Most extraordinarily, the Book of Ruth is about an erasure of the boundary between one's own people and the enemy. Finally, if elsewhere in biblical narrative land is to be conquered and guarded in the cause of nationalism and empire, here for once it is to be shared. For the earth is God's, the fullness of it is God's, and God in this story ceases to be a warrior and becomes a source of life and shelter.

Psalm and Anti-Psalm:
A Personal Interlude

I hate and love. Why, you perhaps might ask.
I don't know. But I feel it, and it is excruciating.

—Catullus

 few days after the destruction of the World Trade Center in New York City on September 11, 2001, the recently inaugurated Poet Laureate of the United States was interviewed by the journalist Sandra Martin. Asked what role poetry might play at such a moment, he replied that for him poetry was a private art and needed a private focus. In a public radio interview on September 11 itself, he suggested that almost any page of any book of poetry would be "speaking for life . . . against what happened today." Or, he said, read the Psalms.[1]

The Psalms? Was he joking?

The Psalms are glorious. No, the Psalms are terrible. No, the Psalms are both glorious and terrible, both attractive and repulsive emotionally and theologically. I read as a poet and a woman, a literary critic and a left-wing Jew who happens to be obsessed with the Bible. And when I read these poems, I experience a split-screen effect: wildly contradictory responses.

To adapt Catullus: I love and hate.

A Joyful Noise

The psalms are overwhelmingly beautiful as poems. They represent the human spirit, my own spirit, in its intimate yearning for a connection with the divine Being who is the source of all being, the energy that creates and sustains the universe. Unlike the portions of the Bible that lay down rules and regulations, and unlike the narratives that tell compelling tales of patriarchs and matriarchs, judges, warriors and kings, but do not tell how they feel, what they think, what it all means to them, the psalms are love poems to God. Since the course of true love never does run smooth, the psalms are poems of emotional turbulence.

Sometimes the psalmist expresses a wonderfully serene, almost childlike faith and trust. "The Lord is my shepherd; I shall not want. He makes me to lie down in green pastures. He leads me beside the still waters. He restores my soul." The ineffable sweetness of this pastoral image surely taps a deep human desire to be relieved of responsibility, including the responsibility of being human. Is that why the twenty-third Psalm is the most popular in the whole psalter? In "He restores my soul," the Hebrew for "my soul" is *nafshi,* a term humans share with animals. It is wonderful, too, that the psalmist does not declare "I am a sheep" or "I am like a sheep," but speaks directly as from the animal soul, the *nefesh,* itself. In Psalm 37 we are advised not to "fret" over evildoers; they are going to disappear, and "the meek shall inherit the earth." All of us who are meek, who feel powerless on earth, can identify with this fantasy. Sometimes a psalm runs a video in my frontal lobe and causes my back to straighten and my lungs to pull in air—"I will lift up my eyes unto the hills, whence cometh my help. My help cometh from the Lord, who made heaven and earth" (121). These two sentences are so physical, but then so metaphysical, shaped like a chiasmus (a kind of word sandwich) but also striking a sequence of registers that expand into larger and larger space: body (eyes), natural environment (vista of hills), cosmos (heaven, earth). I catch my breath every time. I feel confident and alive every time. Commercials for recreational vehicles profiled against a mountain sunrise try to press the same button of exhilaration in me, but something is missing. Commercial culture gives me nothing like this:

> My help cometh from the Lord, who made heaven and earth. He will not suffer thy foot to be moved. He that keepeth thee will not slumber. . . . The Lord is thy keeper. The Lord is thy shade upon thy right hand. The sun shall not smite thee by day nor the moon by night. The Lord shall preserve thee from all evil.

God is connected to nature, as its maker. God is in the hills; God is in the mountains. God made heaven and earth, so you and I are protected by the entire cosmos, which makes us very safe. God even makes it possible to shift pronouns from me to you without a touch of anxiety. And look at the security blanket of language when the psalmist has "behaved and quieted myself, like a child just weaned from his mother. My soul is like a weaned child" (131), which means not a child in the womb or a nursing child, but one who has left those comforts behind, and probably wept for them, but is confident of being loved anyway.

At other moments the psalmist is racked by doubt and self-doubt. "How long wilt thou forget me, O Lord? For ever?" (13). Here is a voice of suffering, complaining, crying out, feeling abandoned, hurt, tormented. "My God, my God, why have you forsaken me? Why art thou so far from helping me, and from the mouth of my roaring?" (22). It seems evident that wicked people prosper in this world, that good people suffer, and that God refuses to intervene. "Why standest thou far off, O Lord? Why hidest thou in time of trouble? The wicked persecute the poor. . . . [The wicked man] boasts of his heart's desire. . . . As for his enemies, he puffeth at them" (10). Or, as we would say, the bad guy blows off anyone who bothers him. "They are enclosed in their own fat, with their mouths they speak proudly" (17). "And they say, How does God know?" (73). "O God, how long shall the adversary reproach? Shall the enemy blaspheme thy name for ever?" (74). Evildoers get away with murder; they are shameless, and the psalmist passionately begs God's help.

Many psalms evoke experiences of being alone, attacked, persecuted, punished. Some beg forgiveness for sin: "Have mercy upon me, O God. . . . a broken spirit and a contrite heart, O God, thou wilt not despise" (51). Many speak from desperation. "Save me, O God, for the waters have come into my soul. I sink in deep mire. The ones that hate me without a cause are more than the hairs of my head" (69). "My days are consumed like smoke. My heart is withered like grass" (102). I recognize the sense of sinking dread, the feeling that my life is meaningless, that my emotions have dried up. The poetry articulates my dread and dryness in exquisite figurative language, which makes it hurt both less, because of the beauty, and more, because of the accuracy. And then the feeling modulates with incredible subtlety. One of my favorite psalms is 42: "As the hart pants after the water brooks, so my soul pants after thee, O God." What a melancholy yet sweet image of the desire for God, the desire of a thirsting animal. The soul, my soul, is *nafshi* again, here. The yearning is as pure as that physical need. But then it turns. "My soul thirsts for God, for the living God. When shall I come and appear before God? My tears have been my meat night and day while they continually say unto me, 'where is thy God?'" It is not simply that I fruitlessly long to be close to God, united with God, but that at the same time, and precisely because everyone knows I go around with this spiritual need, people mock me. Those who do not have my faith or my need, and do not want it, and can live their lives nicely without it, mock me. Evidently it gives them satisfaction to ridicule me. And let me remember that men and women for aeons have been mocked in far worse circumstances than mine: in jail, under interrogation, under torture, at the point of martyrdom. I imagine there was considerable mockery, and self-mockery, in the concentration camps of Europe in the last century.

Then again many psalms express jubilation, celebration, wonder, and awe. "Make a joyful noise unto God, all ye lands" (66) is a tone repeatedly struck. "Sing unto God a new song" (120), with the sense that God is present throughout the cosmos and is everywhere at once awesome and delightful. "Let everything that lives and breathes give praise to the Lord" (150). The Hebrew title for the book of Psalms is *Tehillim,* derived from *hallel,* to praise (cf. the word *hallelujah*), and means Praises:

> Whither shall I go from thy spirit, or whither shall I flee from thy presence? If I ascend up into heaven, thou art there. If I make my bed in hell, behold, thou art there. If I take the wings of the morning and dwell in the uttermost parts of the sea, even there shall thy hand lead me and thy right hand hold me. (139)

This begins with an edge of fear, the suggestion of a wish to escape, but turns out to be very close to love-play, love-teasing, especially in its echo of the sensuousness of the Song of Songs: "his right hand is under my head, and his left hand embraces me." The voice of the psalmist is the voice of one who would like to be experiencing this sublime wonder, this intimacy, this sense of being surrounded by a tenderly loving yet cosmically powerful God, day and night. Of course, it doesn't happen that way, just as it doesn't happen that way in our own relationships. The emotions of the psalms surge and collapse like breaking waves, as they do in our own emotional lives. There is joy and despair and hope and frustration and fear and anger and grief and sorrow and then the desperation breaks like a wave into trust and joy again.

Uncontrollable, unpredictable. Scholars have tried in vain to find an orderly structure in the sequence of psalms because there is very little in the way of rhyme or reason to them. They are not rational; they are intense. Anyone who meditates knows how unruly the mind is. You try to still it and make it serene, and it fails to obey. This is what we find in the psalms as well. They resemble a magnifying glass, that seems to be looking at the presence and withdrawal of God, but in another sense they can be looking at the capacity of the mind to secrete its own calm, and then its inability to grasp that calm for more than moments at a time. What remains constant throughout is faith that God exists, whether present or absent. "The fool says in his heart that there is no God" (14), but, in the world of the psalms, only a fool would think such a thing. In the world of the psalms, God is ultimately our deliverer; we have only to trust. "They that sow in tears shall reap in joy" (126).

All this makes for magnificent poetry, obviously, and of the kind that survives translation in language, time, and space. The Psalms exist in hundreds of languages and form an endless source for Jewish, Christian, and Muslim cultures. The idea of faith, love, and devotion in the Psalms saturates the Gospels, whose early readers would of course have known the Psalms well because they form a central part of Jewish liturgy. When Jesus in the beatitudes says that the meek shall inherit the earth, he repeats the psalmist's wishful thinking. When he declares, "If any one thirst, let him come to me and drink," he takes the trope of spiritual thirst from Psalm 42. When on the cross he cries "My God, my God, why hast thou forsaken me," quoting Psalm 22.1, he is crying out as a Jew in his death as well as in his life.

The psalms have inspired mystics through the centuries and continue to inspire poets beyond the boundaries of conventional religion. Think, for example, of Whitman's insistence on celebrating every jot and tittle of the created world. Or the close of W. H. Auden's elegy on W. B. Yeats, with its parallel death-and-rebirth motif: "Follow, poet, follow right/ To the bottom of the night . . . With your uncomplaining voice/ Still persuade us to rejoice . . . In the prison of his days/ Teach the free man how to praise." How to praise is one great lesson of the Psalms. Literature in English is irrigated by these poems, not only because of the multitude of memorable phrases in the King James Version that I and other poets steal, but also because they are always telling us to celebrate, praise, open ourselves to the universe. That is the task of the poet, or at least I take it to be my task as a poet and a human being, attempting to open myself in praise of an existence that inevitably includes suffering, anguish, pain, despair.

A poem by Sharon Olds typifies the way the psalms can be used in ways that may seem shocking but are perfectly faithful to their spirit. The poem, "Sex Without Love," is an attempt to imagine how they "do it," the people who make love without love:

How do they come to the
come to the come to the God come to the

still waters and not love
the one that came there with them.

Lifted directly from the Twenty-Third Psalm, the poem's
stumbling incredulity assumes that, when we do love the
person we make love with, it is like that moment of blissful
safety in the psalms where we know ourselves to be cared for
by the Lord who is our shepherd.

A Rod of Iron

Magnificent poems. When I read them through the lens of
politics, I shudder at their magnificence. It is perhaps a figure
and ground problem. Let me point out that although there
has been an explosion of scholarly and critical writing about
the Bible by women in the last fifteen or twenty years, almost nothing has been written about the Book of Psalms by
contemporary women scholars. That is rather curious. Part of
the reason, surely, is that unlike books of the Bible such as
Genesis, Exodus, the Song of Songs, the Book of Ruth, or the
Scroll of Esther, or even Proverbs with its stereotyped por-
traits of the evil seductress and the good woman whose price
is above rubies, no women at all appear in the Psalms. No Eve
with her talking snake and her fruit, no laughter of Sarah, no
Miriam with her timbrels and her song.

But the problem runs deeper. We do not take literally the
old idea that the psalms were composed by King David, yet
the psalmist often seems less a generic human than a public
man. A politician, a warrior. The sun may rise in the psalms
like a bridegroom running to meet his bride, but nothing like
domestic life or domestic imagery enters. What I hear, when
I read consciously as a woman with antiwar tendencies, are

the personal meditations and intimate feelings of a man who feels himself to be surrounded by enemies. Are his enemies personal rivals? Are they political or military foes? The categories seem virtually interchangeable. An enemy is an enemy. The psalmist's enemies are *evildoers, workers of iniquity,* and *adversaries.* They are *the proud* and *the heathen.* They *blaspheme* and are *violent.* They oppress the poor and the fatherless. And then again they *persecute* and *lay snares for* the psalmist.

How are we to interpret this motif? If the psalmist is David, then the enemies might include King Saul who through much of Samuel I is trying to hunt down David and kill him. Or the enemies might be the Philistines against whom David waged many battles. But what about us, the readers? Insofar as you and I identify with these poems, our most dangerous and hurtful enemy is probably a family member, a neighbor, a coworker, a boss. Perhaps an unspoken reason for the universal appeal of the Psalms is that ordinary people all over the world feel themselves to be at the mercy of enemies large and small. But here is the rub. In our lives, and the life of history, the animus against personal foes is made to accrue to public ones; the purpose of state propaganda is to take our personal frustration and anger and redirect them against the foes of our rulers. We the people can always be manipulated to hate some demonized Other. At the same time, whatever damage we endure at the hands of those more powerful than ourselves can be taken out on whoever is weaker than ourselves. "Those to whom evil is done/ Do evil in return," as Auden points out in "September 1, 1939," the single poem most widely circulated in the wake of the World Trade Center attack. The interchangability of public and private hostilities is finely mirrored by the ambiguities of the Psalms.

Fascinatingly, in this world of mighty rhetoric, the sins are commonly sins of the tongue. "His mouth is full of cursing and deceit and fraud" (10). They "have sharpened their tongues like a serpent" (140). Their "mouth speaketh vanity" (144). They are foes of Israel, foes of God, and the psalmist wants them destroyed. Is it yearning for goodness and justice on earth that drives his fantasies, is it yearning for vengeance, is it mere hatred of Otherness? Can we necessarily tell the difference? An enemy is an enemy. Ocasionally the imagery of punishment is less than lethal, but it is always urgently physical. "Thou shalt break them with a rod of iron; thou shalt dash them in pieces like a potter's vessel" (2). "Break thou the arm of the wicked and the evil man" (10). "Upon the wicked shall he rain snares, fire and brimstone" (11). "The enemies of the Lord shall be as the fat of lambs: they shall consume; into smoke they shall consume away" (37). "Break their teeth, O God, in their mouth: break out the great teeth of the young lions, O lord. Let them melt away like water. . . . The righteous shall rejoice when he seeth the vengeance: he shall wash his feet in the blood of the wicked" (58). Magnificent poetry. Sublimated aggression, which, like latent energy, is easily converted to action. State propaganda. Psychological projection. All of the above. All.

Part of what makes the dream of punishing the enemy in the Psalms so forceful is the way punishment blooms like a flower from pathos. Poetically, the "turn" of numerous psalms is from devastating grief to its redress, which is sometimes an expectation of deliverance in generalized terms and sometimes the more exciting promise that our enemies will be destroyed. Psalm 137, one of the most evocative in the psalter, speaks from the perspective of the Israelites driven into exile and slavery after the Babylonian destruction of Jerusalem in 587 BCE. In a way it is a typical psalm, full of unpredictable changes in tone. It begins with a picture of a crowd of people carrying their few belongings sitting by a river that is not their home.

> By the waters of Babylon, there we sat down, yea, we
> wept when we remembered Zion. We hanged our harps
> upon the willows in the midst thereof. For there they
> that carried us away captive required of us a song; and
> they that wasted us required of us mirth, saying, Sing
> us one of the songs of Zion.

These extraordinary opening lines, which audiences all over the world today know from Bob Marley's reggae version, convey a scene of conventional beauty—a river with its willows—suffused by a collective sorrow. The sitting down on the ground is extended by tears falling and harps hanging, further images of helplessness. Simultaneously the sitting and the hanging up of harps is also a kind of passive disobedience during a forced march. And is there not a relation between the waters of Babylon and the flowing tears? Then the mood shifts from simple grief to irony. The bitterness of being mocked by those who are stronger, which is such a powerful theme throughout Psalms, is particularly piercing here. "How can we sing the Lord's song in a strange land?" Nothing in poetry so succinctly captures the trauma of exile. Our enemies, who have conquered our land, destroyed our homes and our holy temple and are herding us along, are making fun of us by asking us to sing, in effect, a psalm. The demand is not only cruel but absurd. How can we sing God's song in a foreign land? The Hebrew Bible claims throughout that the children of Israel cannot separate their identity as a people from the land God has given them. This portion of Psalm 137 is like saying not only won't we sing, but we can't sing. Song cannot come out of us if we are not in our home place.

And then comes the moment of the vow. I may be in exile now, but I will never forget. These next lines at once intensify and reverse the grief at captivity: "If I forget thee,

O Jerusalem, may my right hand forget her cunning. May my tongue cleave to the roof of my mouth if I remember not Jerusalem above my chief joy." Notice the shift from first person plural "we" to the singular "I," and how the hand that acts, the tongue that converses and sings, become subject to the mind that swears not to become assimilated to the alien culture. I do everything with my right hand, so these lines are asking to be paralyzed if I fail to cherish the memory of Jerusalem above every other pleasure in my life. And in fact the passion of the exile for the homeland has remained alive in Judaism for two thousand years, since the destruction of the second temple in the year 70 of the common era. Jews in diaspora ritually promise each other "next year in Jerusalem" at the close of every year's Passover feast.

The poignance of the vow in Psalm 137 is extraordinary. It signals a spiritual triumph over the initial scene of powerlessness, as if declaring that Babylon may capture bodies but not souls. At this point the psalmist, turning to God, reminds God of the destruction of his own sacred city: "Remember, O Lord, the children of Edom in the day of Jerusalem; who said, Rase it, rase it, even to the foundation thereof." Finally comes the poem's prophetic conclusion: "O daughter of Babylon, who art to be destroyed, happy shall he be, that rewardeth thee as thou hast served us. Happy shall he be, that taketh and dasheth thy little ones against the stones."

And there we have it, human history, the justification of every blood feud, every literal dashing of children's heads against walls by conquering armies, guerilla armies, occupying forces, terrorist suicide bombers, Arab and Jew, Serb and Bosnian, Hutu and Tutsi, Irish Protestants and Irish Catholics, Buddhist and Hindu in Sri Lanka, Hindu and Muslim throughout the Indian subcontinent, the Shining Path in Peru, to name a few current instances. Not to mention the

Crusades, the Inquisition, the burning of heretics at the stake, the religious wars of sixteenth- and seventeenth-century England and Europe, the pogroms, and the holocaust. The righteous, with God on their side, joyously washing their feet in the blood of the wicked. The righteous, confident that they, and they alone, know God's wishes and are the only ones pure enough to carry out God's will. Osama Bin Laden, shortly after the September 11, 2001 attack that destroyed the World Trade Center, issued a statement broadcast throughout the Islamic world. Is not the rhetoric chillingly familiar?

> Praise be to God and we beseech Him for help and Forgiveness. We seek refuge with the Lord. . . . He whom God guides is rightly guided but he whom God leaves to stray, for him wilt thou find no protector to lead him to the right way.

> I witness that there is no God but God and Mohammed is His slave and Prophet.

> God Almighty hit the United States at its most vulnerable spot. He destroyed its greatest buildings. Praise be to God. Here is the United States. It was filled with terror from its north to its south and from its east to its west. Praise be to God.

> They champion falsehood, support the butcher against the victim, the oppressor against the innocent child. May God mete them the punishment they deserve.[2]

A handwritten document left behind by a leader among the hijackers, Mohammed Atta, urges the prospective hijacker/martyr: "You should pray, you should fast. You should ask

God for guidance. . . . Purify your heart and clean it from all
earthly matters." Among the prayers: "O God, open all doors
for me. O God, who answers prayers and answers those who
ask you, I am asking you for your help. . . . God, I trust in
you. God, I lay myself in your hands."[3]

The Psalms are the prototype in English of devotional poetry and possibly of lyric poetry in general. Let nobody say that
poetry makes nothing happen. Let nobody say that poetry cannot or should not be political. We have this model before us.

Jews, Christians, and Muslims, and pagans before us,[4]
have worshiped a God—have created a God to worship—
who is both tender and violent. God is father, judge, warrior,
mighty arm, rock, redeemer, and (with a little help from his
friends) destroyer of the godless, which in practice can mean
anyone I take to be my enemy. Is there any way to circum-
vent this conclusion? A famous sermon by the German theologian Dietrich Bonhoeffer, written in 1937 at the brink of
World War II, in which he died a martyr of the resistance
to Hitler, tries to rescue Psalm 58, "this frightful psalm of
vengeance," by claiming that it is not really we sinners who
"are able to pray this psalm." Psalm 58 is the one in which the
enemy's teeth are to be knocked out and the righteous are to
wash their feet in the blood of the wicked. The speaker of the
psalm, says Bonhoefer, is King David, or, rather, Jesus Christ
praying from within David—for "only he who is totally without sin can pray like that." We sinners must entrust vengeance
to God and endure suffering "without a thought of hate, and
without protest." Moreover, if we shudder at the image of the
righteous splashing about in the blood of the guilty, we must
understand that the death sentence has already been enacted
on Jesus, "the Savior who died for the godless, struck down
by God's revenge," that the "bloodstained Savior" redeems
whoever prostrates himself at the Cross. Jesus, then, is both

the psalm's author and its victim; the true Christian is not responsible. Still, Bonhoeffer's solution perpetuates a familiar rhetoric of "the godless," as if we could be certain who they are, and supports a vehemently traditional view of God as chief officer of retribution.[5] In effect, Bonhoeffer recommends that good Christians should avoid guilt and leave the punishing of sinners to God. It sounds, though I hesitate to say so, like Pilate washing his hands. In actuality, Bonhoeffer became involved in the conspiracy of German officers to assassinate Hitler and was hanged in the concentration camp at Flossenbürg on April 9, 1945, one of four members of his immediate family to die at the hands of the Nazi regime.

A beautiful essay by Kathleen Norris, "The Paradox of the Psalms,"[6] takes another approach toward their violence. Norris writes of what she learned during a yearlong residence at a Benedictine convent, where the Psalms are the liturgical mainstay, sung or recited at morning, noon and evening prayer. "How in the world," she asks, "can we read . . . these angry and often violent poems from an ancient warrior culture, [that] seem overwhelmingly patriarchal, ill tempered, moralistic?" She answers that they reflect emotional reality, that the pain in them is essential for praise, that the psalms are full of anger because "anger is one honest reaction to pain," that women who are trained to deny pain and anger—including Benedictine women—may find their expression healthy, and that "as one sister explained, the 'enemies' vilified in the cursing psalms are best seen as 'my own demons, not enemies out there.'"

Of Psalm 137, Norris points out that it has a special poignance for women who experience the journey from girlhood to an adulthood that demands prettiness and niceness as a journey to exile. It also "expresses the bitterness of colonized people everywhere . . . the speaker could be one of today's refugees or exiles, an illegal alien working for far less than minimum wage, a slave laborer in China." The vision of brutal vengeance at its close, "O Babylon, . . . happy is he who repays you the ills you brought on us, happy is he who shall dash your children on the rock," should come as no surprise, she observes; it is "the fruit of human cruelty." She goes on to say that psalms such as this ask us to recognize our own capacity for vengeance and to see it as "a potentially deadly vice" that may be "so consuming that not even the innocent are spared." We should, Norris says, pray over it. Good. But do the vengeance fantasies in the psalms ask to be read this way? Or is it not rather Norris's rather special temperament that chooses so to read them? Aren't the vengeance fantasies in fact endorsed in the poems' theological framework? Endorsed, that is, by God? And, incidentally, is vengeance morally acceptable if it punishes "the guilty" and reprehensible only if it strikes "the innocent"? If so, we return to the sticky question of how guilt and innocence are to be determined, and the likelihood that "the guilty" and "my enemies" will be mysteriously identical.

We may twist on the hook as we will. Once we have bitten the bait of the psalms we are in the power of a vision that mirrors our minds. The character of God in these splendid poems is also our projection, deny it as we may. We create him in our image and attribute holiness and power to him. In "Notes on God's Violence" Catherine Madsen advocates facing the possibility that the biblical God's character "alternates between tender care and ferocious brutality, between limitless creation and wholesale wreckage," not because the biblical God rewards nice people and punishes bad ones, but because "the violence of the universe [is] at every point congruent with its nurturance" and because "Hebrew monotheism sets up one source for good and evil, one responsible will from which they both derive."[7]

The God who speaks to Job out of the whirlwind, that explosion of sublime amoral creativity, is the God of the

Psalms, but with the veil of righteousness removed. Can one love such a God? If one refuses, then does praise too dry up? If one denies God's violence, however, is that not a kind of blasphemy? Stephen Mitchell, the brilliant translator of the Book of Job, recognizes the Voice from the whirlwind as embodying "the clarity, the pitilessness, of nature and of all great art."[8] Mitchell rightly points out how closely this vision of Job resembles the magnificent and terrifying play of divine creation and destruction revealed to Arjuna at the climax of the *Bhagavad Gita*. He quotes Blake's *Marriage of Heaven and Hell:* "The roaring of lions, the howling of wolves, the raging of the stormy sea, and the destructive sword, are portions of eternity too great for the eye of man."[9] Yet I once walked into a bookstore in Berkeley at a moment when Mitchell was reading his versions of Psalms, and was appalled to hear him omit the close of Psalm 137, letting the poem end with the image of Jerusalem as the exile's chief joy, instead of the image of the Babylonian child's head being dashed against a rock. I thought: Has New Age sentimental niceness claimed another victim? Is he trying to convert the Psalms to Buddhism?[10] Is he trying to castrate God? Who does he think he is fooling?

Why does the poet laureate of America, after terrorism has destroyed the World Trade Center and several thousand human lives in New York City, claim that poetry is about personal and not political matters? And why on earth does he cite the Psalms as "against" acts of terror?

Wrestling with Divinity

My poems wrestle with the need of God, the violence of God. I should rather say I that let these matters attack and wrestle with my poems.

In 1999 I find myself working on a manuscript provision-
ally entitled "The Space of This Dialogue," after a sentence
of Paul Celan, "Only in the space of this dialogue does that
which is addressed take form and gather around the I who is
addressing it." The experience is not so much of writing as of
receiving. The poems arrive intermittently, and I have undertaken not to tell them what to say. They often address God,
not expecting a response. Early in the process I write down
some lines and call them "psalm." They are more like an anti-
psalm. They say this:

> I am not lyric any more
> I will not play the harp
> for your pleasure
>
> I will not make a joyful
> noise to you, neither
> will I lament
>
> for I know you drink
> lamentation, too,
> like wine
>
> so I dully repeat
> you hurt me
> I hate you
>
> I pull my eyes away from the hills
> I will not kill for you
> I will never love you again
>
> unless you ask me [11]

What I recognize in the poem is my resistance to a God who deals cruelly with us and still demands our praise. What the final line tells me is that I want to stop resisting. Perhaps I am like one of those abused woman who keeps forgiving her abuser. You read about them: they phone the police and then hide their bruises and refuse to press charges.

Another poem ventriloquizes a pious voice that could emerge from any monotheistic religion and concludes with a last line that is, alas, a vast understatement:

> One of these days
> oh one of these days
> will be a festival and a judgment
> and our enemies will be thrown
> into the pit while we rejoice
> and sing hymns
>
> Some people actually think this way

Later in the manuscript, writing during the 1999 bombing of Kosovo in the former Yugoslavia—remembering that this war of Christian against Muslim is typical of religious wars through the ages, in which God is the gun with which we shoot our enemy—I ask God what he is thinking. The question precipitates a dialogue:

> *the spot of black paint*
> *in the gallon of white*
> *makes it whiter*
>
> *so the evil impulse*
> *is part of you*
> *for a reason*

what reason

greater wilder holiness

*****

so perhaps you want us to understand
it throbs also in you
like leavening

you want us to love that about you
even if you pray that your attribute of mercy
may overcome your attribute of wrath

you want us always to love the evil also
the death-wish also
the bread of hate

because we are your image
confess you prize
the cruel theater of it

An ancient rabbinic story describes God praying in the ru-
ins of the destroyed temple. For what, it is asked, does God
pray? He prays that his attribute of mercy will overcome his
attribute of justice; my poem slightly alters the story. More
painfully, the unnamed responding voice makes a declaration
I cannot deny. It brings me to my knees. It sickens me. I am
very well aware that I, like just about everyone else I know,
rubberneck at traffic accidents. I am outraged by, and avidly
read about and discuss, the horrors of war, torture, the wickedness of congress, the Administration, oil interests, anyone
whose politics or moral principles deviate from my own. As

Elizabeth Bishop says in her poem to Marianne Moore, "we can bravely deplore." And we all enjoy deploring, don't we? Later still, to my surprise, appear poems such as this, which is again entitled "Psalm":

> I endure impure periods
> when I cannot touch you
>
> or even look at you
> you are a storm I would be electrocuted
>
> by your approach then I feel some sort of angelic laughter
> like children behind a curtain
>
> come, I think
> you are at my fingertips my womb
>
> you are the wild driver of my vehicle
> the argument in my poem
>
> nothing between us
> only breath

Where did that come from? I cannot imagine. I feel myself to be an aperture through which the words arrive. Like the biblical psalms, mine seem to be love poems to God. But I cannot justify my love.

ECCLESIASTES AS WITNESS

Happiness and the absurd are two sons of the same earth.
They are inseparable.

—ALBERT CAMUS, *THE MYTH OF SISYPHUS*

T he most brilliantly pessimistic tract of all time, a dense mix of prose and poetry, the biblical book of Ecclesiastes contains a treasury of quotations rivaling Shakespeare. Consider how many turns of phrase have their origin in the King James Version of it. "Vanity of vanities, all is vanity" is its opening salvo. "The sun also rises" gives a title to Hemingway, "remembrance of things past" gives one to Proust, and "the house of mirth" gives one to Edith Wharton. "There is nothing new under the sun," "The race is not to the swift," and "A living dog is better than a dead lion," are among its many pungent sentences. In Ecclesiastes we also find "cast your bread upon the waters," "eat, drink and be merry," and "for everything there is a season." As a store of pure wisdom, the book is by common agreement unequalled.

But what is wisdom? Should reading this book make us feel depressed? Exhilerated? Agitated? Or serene? Does it ask us to believe that this life is the only one we should expect, or does it ask us to trust in an afterlife? Is the God who is invoked some three dozen times in the text in any way benevolent? Is he even real? Did one author write the skeptical bits that I applauded, in the days of my youth, and another the pious bits that I elided from consciousness?

Commentary tosses up large disagreements. The text is pious and skeptical. It was composed by a single, or two, or plural authors, or it was a patchwork cobbled together by an editor.[1] It is a dialogue with the self. It is an argument between despair and hope. It is essentially Epicurean, although "apikorus" later becomes the Hebrew word for heretic. It is essentially Stoic. Its genre, fictional autobiography, goes back to Akkadian literature. It represents the Sadducee position as opposed to the Pharisee.

The author is "the Hebrew Lao Tse."

Like a Buddhist, he recognizes that life is inseperable from suffering and advocates detachment from desire and the pleasures of "ordinary mind."

He is the first empiricist.

He is the first pragmatist.

He is the first existentialist.

Like Einstein, he likes to point out how little we know of the laws of the universe.

He is the first postmodernist writer.

Three Problems

Three problems about this book particularly fascinate me. First, the author's identity is an enigma wrapped in a mystery. The book begins by calling itself "The words of Qoheleth, son of David, king in Jerusalem." The latter part of the sentence points obviously to David's son Solomon, and as The Song of Songs was traditionally held to be the creation of King Solomon's lusty youth and the Book of Proverbs that of his prudent maturity, so Ecclesiastes was believed to be the product of a bitter old age in which Solomon foresaw that his kingdom would come to ruin under his rash son Jereboam. Medieval scholars debated whether Solomon should be seen as the wisest of men seeking further wisdom or as a monarch whose corruption cost his realm. But scholars today agree that none of the books attributed to Solomon could have been written by him and that Ecclesiastes is a work of wisdom literature influenced by Hellenistic culture, composed probably in the third century BCE, half a millennium after the monarch's lifetime. But the persona of Qoheleth remains a mystery. How, in the first place, should the name that appears in the first part of that opening sentence be translated?

"Qoheleth" appears nowhere else in the Bible, as either a noun or a proper name or a title. It is not the name of any king in Chronicles. It derives from a Hebrew term meaning "assembly" or "gathering," and so it may mean "one who addresses an assembly." Ecclesiastes, the Greek translation of Qoheleth, is the title used in all standard English translations, including Jewish ones, but nothing about this text implies an institutional church, still less a priest. Qoheleth might mean one who collects sayings, or gathers wisdom, hence the King James usage "the Preacher." Some translations call him "the Teacher." Both terms misleadingly suggest a degree of consistency, objectivity, and solidity of thought and emotion, which the text fails to sustain.

Yet another suggestion is that the book should be called "The Testimony of Solomon," capturing the possible legal and religious connotations of assembly, but this seems excessively formal for the author's exclamatory and spiky style. Besides, "testimony" is a distinctly masculine term (a cognate is testicles; men covered their testicles with their right hand when taking an oath, before courts had testaments to swear on), while Qoheleth is a feminine noun in its form—for reasons no scholarship explains.[2] But remembering how often the author speaks of *seeing,* and how his favorite phrases include "I saw under the sun" and "I said in my heart," I would like to call the author the Witness. I think here of Paul Celan's question, "Who will bear witness for the witness?" and of what today we name, after the cascade of horrors in the twentieth century, the poetry of witness.

A second problem is the famous refrain. "Vanity of vanities" echoes through centuries of English literature and speech. Samuel Johnson's "The Vanity of Human Wishes" depends on the phrase, as does the opening of Robert Browning's "The Bishop Orders His Tomb," "Vanity, saith the Preacher, vanity." The phrase gives us Tom Wolfe's novel *The Bonfire of the Vanities* and provides the understood but missing part of a volume of poems by Robert Hass, *Human Wishes.*

The excellence of the King James translation "vanity" as key to the world-view of the Witness lies in the term's double meaning, signifying both vain self-conceit and meaningless void. But the Hebrew *hevel* is even more subtly layered, and carries even more pathos in its empty cup. *Hevel* may mean "vapor" or "mist," with a connotation of "breath," and so a suggestion simultaneously of that which is essential to life, and that which is utterly ephemeral. It may mean "wind." It may mean "emptiness" or "void," in a sense adjacent to Taoist or Buddhist concepts of emptiness. The rabbi Rami Shapiro describes his excitement when a college friend rushed into his room exclaiming that what was usually translated "vanity" really meant "emptiness."[3] It is also the Hebrew for Abel, the name of the first murdered man in scripture, a man favored by God but unlucky, whose brother was not his keeper, the man whose whole life was mist.

Vanity is an abstraction, and the Hebrew *hevel* is not. Not quite, though close. As close as a breath. Something perhaps close to nothing, but not quite nothing. A reality, not an abstraction. A metaphor afloat at the edge of what is mentally graspable. To this word, this name, Qoheleth keeps returning. Often he pairs it with another phrase, equally ambiguous in meaning. "I have seen all the works that are done under the sun," he says, "all *hevel* and a striving after wind." Or, in other translations, pursuit of wind. Striving after wind means trying to catch the wind, as Thomas Wyatt puts it in a poem about failing to capture a desireable woman and finally quitting: "Since in a net I seek to hold the wind." The Hebrew *r'ut* literally means "tending" or "herding," from the root *ra'ah* "to shepherd," so the sense is something like the idea of herding cats. Frustrating, yes, but less tragic than comic. To add to the ambiguity, wind and spirit are the same word in Hebrew, just as spirit and breath are the same in Latin.[4] *Ruach. Spiritus.* Trying to catch, capture, herd the wind? Or the spirit? And if so, what spirit? Whose? In Genesis 1.2, *ruach elohim* hovers (or broods) on the face of the waters. Perhaps it is significant that *ruach* is a female noun, perhaps not. The phrase, or a variant of it, occurs again and again in the text, and it is often impossible to tell whether Qoheleth is talking about the failed efforts of others, or his own, or both. All human effort is an effort to control the wind, to control the spirit, the Witness says. This is less accusatory than "vanity," more poignant, more absurd. In the space created by these phrases we may find a door that, when passed through, opens straight into the existentialism of Camus.

Finally, what is God doing in Ecclesiastes? He resembles the God of the rest of the Hebrew Bible very little. He is neither the God of my fathers, nor the God of battles. Israel concerns him not at all. Neither ritual nor law interests him. He is not the personal Jahweh, the one who makes and keeps the Covenant, but *Elohim,* the remote-control universal One who in Genesis speaks the universe into existence and creates the earthling, Adam, as a pun on *adamah,* earth.[5] This plural form of the divine name, which in pagan contexts simply means "the gods," tells us that he contains a stubborn residue of other and older religions in which he was either androgynous, which he becomes again in Kaballa, or a divine couple, or perhaps an assembly of deities. Ontogeny recapitulates phylogeny. The text seems to represent God the way Hellenistic philosophers do in the same period, as some combination of abstraction, personified force, and actual divine being. Yet moral questions hover around the edges of this representation like a swarm of almost-invisible mayflies.

Without attempting to solve the many riddles in Ecclesiastes, I want to look at the way these three issues of the persona of the writer, the recurrent reminder that all is mist, and the idea of God, play out in multiple potential ways in the text and how they connect with what is *not* ambiguous in it: the repeated insistence that our ridiculous "I," our experience of life's vain windy-soulful mistiness, and the monster or puppet-master we call God, together constitute an invitation to enjoy ourselves.

The First Person Singular

Qoheleth, whoever he is, invents the autobiographical "I" of western literature, glamorizes it, and ridicules it, all at the same time. Characters certainly exist elsewhere in the Bible and in the epics and drama of classical literature. But apart from short lyrics, self-conscious authorial subjectivity does not exist before Ecclesiastes. It has been argued that the form is anticipated in the royal "autobiographies" of several ancient rulers. But compare the crude account of Sargon—"Aggi the water-drawer raised me as his adopted son. Aggi the water-drawer set me to his gardening. During my garden work Ishtar loved me so that I ruled fifty-five years as king. I took over and governed the black-headed people"—or Idrini's "I constructed a house with the property, goods, possessions and valuables that I brought down from Hatti. I made my throne like the throne of kings, my sons like their sons and my friends like their friends. I made my inhabitants who were in the midst of my land dwell in better dwellings"[6]—with the vibrant and rasping interiority of Qoheleth:

> I Qoheleth was king over Israel in Jerusalem. And I gave my heart to seek and search by wisdom all that happens under heaven. A bad business that God gave the sons of men to busy themselves with. I observed all the happenings under the sun, and I found that all is *hevel* and pursuit of *ruach*. . . . I said to myself in my heart,[7] Here I am, richer and wiser than any that ruled before me over Jerusalem, and my heart has understood great wisdom and knowledge. And I set my heart to know wisdom and to know madness and folly. And I learned that this too is pursuit of *ruach*. (1.12–17)

The tone is at once grandiose, mordant, and poignant from the outset. An unflinching recognition of the transience of all things in the natural world, especially human life and its accomplishments, combines with a point-by-point deflation of traditional values. Nothing is new under the sun. The speaker has tested both wisdom and folly and found both to be *hevel,* transient mist, vanity, vapor. He has tried drunken madness, acquired untold wealth, successfully engaged in great building projects, agricultural enterprises and public works, gotten himself flocks and herds, silver and gold treasures of kings and provinces, slaves and entertainers, withholding from his eyes nothing they ask for, enjoying it all—the tale of course designed to make the audience's tongue hang out as the ultimate in glamor—but ultimately concluding that all is *hevel* and pursuit of *ruach* and that there is no profit under the sun because he does not know who will succeed to all this wealth. As soon as he declares that "wisdom is better than folly as light is better than darkness," he recalls that the same fate awaits the wise and the fool, and wonders what profit it is to him to be so wise. Wise men die as well as fools, and nobody remembers they existed (2.1–19).

The whole passage is clotted with obsessive repetition. Qoheleth cannot stop harping on *yitrot,* "profit" and pointing out the worthlessness of *amal amalti,* which might be translated "the work I worked," "the labor in which I labored," "the toil in which I toiled," or "the gain I gained." He is like a Wall Street tycoon or a media celebrity facing the grim reaper. Over and over again this phrase or some variant of it reappears. In what was probably a third-century BCE Palestine under Ptolemaic rule, Qoheleth inhabited a world like ours, dominated by the marketplace. His profit motif is our profit motive. If he is cynical, his cynicism should sound familiar to us.[8]

But what follows from this apparent dead end of thought? Shortly after announcing "I hated life" (2.17), Qoheleth is concluding that "nothing is good for a man but that he should eat and drink, and allow his soul enjoyment in his work,[9] which is from the hand of God" (2.24); soon after that comes a relaxation of tension in the beautiful passage of 3.1–8, that begins "To everything there is a season." Here the thought has balance and grace and ease; we can breathe deeply as the pairs dance by, "A time to be born and a time to die; a time to plant and a time to root up what is planted; a time to kill and a time to heal. . . . a time to love and a time to hate;

a time of war and a time of peace." The passage from 3.1 to 3.8 is like a turbulent body of water that grows calm and can serenely reflect trees, sky, clouds. The passage brims with harmony—which does not last.[10] Nothing lasts, in the stream of Qoheleth's consciousness; all the more does his consciousness faithfully mirror a world driven by time, chance, rolling suns, whirling winds, an endless water cycle, dying generations, and a class structure.

Qoheleth in effect invents for western civilization the thrill of disillusion. A bracing exhilaration rises from his caustic treatment of everyone else's values. Hard work, wealth, possessions, power, children, ancestors, the quest for knowledge and understanding—forget it. Forget them. In the face of death, which takes wise man and fool alike, man and beast alike— and nobody knows if man's soul rises up to heaven and the beast's goes down, more likely both turn to dust—what is the point? What's the profit? Out there in the world, it's a crapshoot. "The race is not to the swift, nor the battle to the strong, nor bread to the wise, nor riches to men of understanding" (9.11). God puts a craving for knowledge in our hearts, yet he has frustrated us in advance by making the world far too mysterious for us to understand. Finally, human society is ridden by envy and oppression, for which there is no comfort because the wicked often enjoy long and happy lives. So much for the world we live in. Less often noticed is Qoheleth's equally caustic attitude toward himself as he records the twists and turns of mood, the exasperating ricochet of emotions that are the consequence of being an "I." Especially self-mocking, it seems to me, are the way "profit" keeps yanking his chain, and the way the "wisdom" on which he prides himself keeps ending in the cul-de-sac of an irritated shrug. Behold the glory and the absurdity of possessing a self and self-knowledge. Best-case scenario is also worst-case: only the very privileged and the very clever are subject to the ennui Qoheleth explores with such fascination.

"I set my heart," he announces. "I said in my heart," "I saw," "I returned and saw," "I returned and saw under the sun." We are listening to a man talking to himself. We are listening to the way a mind skids and loops, when it has the privilege and leisure to do so. We are watching the little electric charges travel the neural traintracks in their compulsive little circles. This is what Buddhists call the monkey mind. It is what we hear it doing when we are *trying* to be tranquil. The Buddha when he sat under the banyan tree, another son of privilege, probably heard something similar for the first couple of his seven years.

The Witness wants us to know that he is not merely theorizing, he is an empiricist. His claims are nailed down by "I." Yet we also recognize that his "I" is a fiction, a thought-experiment. Conceivably, Qoheleth's earliest readers knew this, at least half-consciously, as well as we do. Speaking "in the name of" a revered antecedent is, in rabbinic writings, a conventional way of doing homage to a teacher, or perhaps a way of saying that one is inhabited by the thoughts of that teacher. From here it is but a short hop to the recognition that "I" is at all times a fiction, a trouble-making construction with which we are all afflicted. Every mystical tradition on earth tells us the same thing: Christianity, Sufism, the Upanishads, Buddhism. Buddha's first Noble Truth is that life is suffering, and his second is that suffering is due to attachment, including our attachment to an idea of ourselves. Exactly. Kabbala, too, posits the human self as a complicated structure of ten sefirot—or, alternatively, as *ayin,* nothingness.[11] Getting past the "I" is of course easier said than done, and Qoheleth doesn't do it either, except in brief flashes, like the rest of us. He is not *theorizing* the entrapment of ego; he is *illustrating* it.

What is the function here of the occasional intermittent lines that sound so conventionally rocklike in Qoheleth's stream of consciousness, the prudent ones that could have been lifted out of the book of normative and plodding Proverbs? Whole stretches of the text of Ecclesiastes give advice. "When you make a vow to God, do not delay to pay it. . . . Better not to vow than vow and not pay" (5.4–5). "The patient in spirit is better than the proud in spirit" (7.8). "Wisdom strengthens the wise man more than ten rulers of the city" (7.19). "He who digs a pit will fall into it" (10.8). "Do not curse the king, even in your thought; do not curse the rich, even in your bedroom; for a bird of the air may carry your voice, and a bird in flight may tell the thing" (10.20). According to some commentators, these sayings reinforce Qoheleth's essential piety and propriety. According to others, they are targets for his irony. For yet others, they are interpolations by later editors.[12] We might also see them simply as part of the dreary and necessary mental baggage that turns up in a mind that is attempting to look at itself. "I" is a great king, a seeker after wisdom, an adventurer, a compost heap.

Blowing in the Wind

Vanity, mist, vapor, breath, spirit, wind. We want to be truly alive before we die. We want to arrive at the moments that exist outside of death, of change, of time. Art and philosophy urgently point that way, gesturing beyond time into timelessness (miscalled eternity) and the space beyond space (miscalled infinity). We know well enough that linear extension (more hours and years, more miles and leaps from galaxy to galaxy) is a childish fantasy (like the fantasy of more and more money) that is not what the mature mind asks. The mind asks another dimension. It asks time and space to *stop*.

Here is another thought experiment, or rather an actuality. A best-case scenario as sweet as any. It brims with beauty, the world, it and I are bursting, as I cross a footbridge on a cold January night after a poetry reading, pushing my bicycle across the wooden slats like a good citizen because the sign says "cyclists dismount" and gazing rapturously down at the dark river water with the lights sailing in it and the swans more or less at rest in their usual location where people come to feed them in daytime. Water, water, gratifying and comforting element, gently moving in the cold. Iron railing up here. Stable brick rowhouses on the other side, like a promise of decent prosperity, time without end, only a few cars going by because it is so late, and the winter sky, and the riverbank itself with its empty benches and the willow hanging over— and the eye, that most complex and subtle organ, greediest portion of the body, greedier than mouth or genitals, brims with its own seeing, takes in the world at every fraction of a second, an infinite picture—and sends it where? Where "I" want hands or words to capture and hold it and cannot. Isn't this infinitely frustrating and infinitely laughable?

Mephistopheles tells Faust that if he lapses from the enjoyment of any moment and says to it "Stay, thou art so fair," he forfeits his soul. Mephistopheles will seize it. We know that whenever something is forbidden it will happen; that is story logic. Faust ought to be damned. But Goethe turns tragedy to comedy by, of all things, letting Faust turn to work.

When I am miserable I want the moment to go away, but it clings tenaciously, or more accurately I wrap it stubbornly around myself like a winter coat. I brood that nobody loves me; I rehearse bitter sentences I could fling at my enemies.

Ah, but the truth is I do not deserve to be loved; I'm a bad mother, daughter, teacher, friend, citizen. I don't do enough to help erase poverty, injustice, and war. I am incompetent, stupid, a failure. Or alternatively I am brilliant and unappreciated; other people have prizes and fame that I should be getting. And so on. Around the loop. Being depressed is shameful and depressing. That I apparently choose to make the barbed wire of depression my security blanket is rather funny when I come to think of it—and *if* I can come to think of it, do I not notice the barbed wire loosening, like an involuntary smile? On the other hand, when I am rejoicing, that is when my heart and eyes are open and stars are falling into my cup, I brim shiveringly and want a lover to share the beauty, or I want to catch it in my fisherwoman's net and write it down—keep it alive that way? pass it along that way, to the unknown lovers of the world? I want the moment to *stay,* which it never does. Am I damned, then, or do small effervescent bubbles of comedy rise through me at the thought of my own foolishness?

I believe I hear Qoheleth laughing at himself. He laughs at the joke of having a self that inevitably ties itself into knots. He derides the labor in which he labors, in which his trapped language writhes with baffled disbelief, thus entangling itself ever more thoroughly. The Witness both exhibits the behavior of the profit-seeking "I" who keeps working for material and intellectual goods, and condemns that behavior, at the same time. Or is this a condemnation?

If *hevel* is "vanity," then yes, the tone is one of bitter contempt. If "mist" or "vapor," then it is a tone of compassion, perhaps bemused compassion. If *hevel* is the name of the first man who was killed by his brother, the name we translate into English as "Abel," then what's called for is grief. Over and over again, the identical and original grief. After the first death there is no other. For imagine that all experience, all work, all profit from work, all wisdom, folly, desire, all our possessions, all our knowledge, are like a man whose offering is approved by God and who is about to be killed by his brother. That innocent man, whose life is but a breath. At one point, contemplating "all the oppression that is done under the sun, and look! the tears of the oppressed, but they have no comforter; power is on the side of the oppressors," Qoheleth cannot bear it. He praises the long dead more than the living and declares better than both the one "who has never existed, who has not seen the evil work that is done under the sun" (4.1–3). Later, imagining a man (an alter ego?) who "begets a hundred children and lives many years, so that the days of his years are many, but his soul is not satisfied with goodness," Qoheleth exclaims, "I say a stillborn child, though it had no burial, is better than he, for it comes in *hevel* and departs in darkness, and its name is covered with darkness, though it has not seen or known the sun, it has more rest than that man" (6.3–5). It is a painful self-sentencing. Like Job, however, who similarly curses the day he was born, Qoheleth stays alive as if waiting for something. For if *hevel* is indeed the breath of life, or the emptiness within meditation, then it may open the soul's contemplative door to a place of extraordinary serenity.

What disperses mist is sunshine, and the sun of enlightenment shines periodically through Qoheleth's mist. For Qoheleth is no Hamlet. Although he may say "I hated my life," or "I hated all my labor," there is no lapse of energy and vigor in his tone, and, although he claims (along with the Greek tragedians) that it is better not to be born, there is no toying with suicide. On the contrary, what seems to follow from the meaninglessness and brevity of life is a resolution to enjoy it. "There is nothing better for a man than that he should eat and drink and that he should make his soul enjoy good in his labor. This . . . is from the hand of God" (2.24).

No sooner does the Witness question "What profit does a man have . . ." than he notes the beauty and mystery of God's creation. Having observed that men are no better than beasts, he concludes that "a man should rejoice." A long passage hammering home the sad inevitability of death, and the loss of all the loves, hates, and jealousies we experience in the world, is followed by an even longer exhortation: "Go, eat your bread with joy . . . live joyfully with the woman whom you love all the days of the life of your *hevel.* . . . Whatsoever your hand finds to do, do it with your might; for there is no work . . . in the grave to which you go" (9.7–10). Consciousness of our doom, according to Qoheleth, should lead us to conduct our lives with both wisdom and energy.

Nowhere are these injunctions more poignantly stated than in the beautiful lines of chapter 12, near the close of the book, with their mysteriously symbolic evocation of mortality. The ubiquitous "I" has now disappeared. Metaphor has appeared in its place. The tone is strangely calm and ample, while the topic is distinctly and unsentimentally grim: the misery of old age, the collapse of virility, the advent of blindness, deafness, weakness, fearfulness, death itself.

> Remember your creator in the days of your youth, while
>   the evil days come not, nor the days arrive, when
>   you shall say, I have no pleasure in them; before the
>   sun, and the light, and the moon, and the stars, are
>   darkened,
> and the clouds return after the rain;
> When the guards of the house shall tremble
> and the strong men bow down
> and the grinders cease because they are few,
> and those that look out from the windows grow dim,
> and the doors to the street are shut,

when the voice of the grinding mill is low
and one starts up at the voice of the bird,
and all the daughters of song are brought low,
When one is afraid of what is high
and there are terrors on the road,
and the almond tree blossoms,
the grasshopper is a burden
and desire fails,
for man goes to his eternal home
and the mourners go about the streets.
Before the silver cord is snapped
and the golden bowl is broken
and the pitcher is broken at the spring
and the wheel broken at the cistern
and the dust returns to the earth as it was
and the spirit returns to God who gave it,
mist of mists, says the Witness,
all is mist.

The effect of this blossoming of sensuous language is as if a film, just before its final frames, suddenly changed from black and white to technicolor. Commentators have vainly attempted to nail down the "meaning" of all the metaphors. Yes, the grinders are teeth, and the ones who look out of the windows are eyes. The silver cord is perhaps umbilical, the golden bowl is perhaps womblike, or perhaps a skull. It can also be claimed that the passage allegorizes the loss of sexuality, as *anshe hechayil*, strong men or men of valor may mean virile men, *hatochenet* are female grinders (and grinding elsewhere implies sex), *harovot ba-aruvot* are females who look through the windows—the same image used for the seductress in Proverbs 7.6. Talmud sees the grasshopper line as an allusion to impotence.[13] But in a sense, the most significant meaning of the passage as a whole is that its imagery gives intense pleasure. And the pleasure inevitably adheres to the motive of all these metaphors: mortality. This is what poetry does: ready or not, it blesses whatever it touches.

Some say that Ecclesiastes is read at the feast of Succoth, a harvest holiday, to teach people to despise mundane matters as vanity. Others say that it is read then because Succoth is a season of joy, and Qoheleth praises the joy of those who do not pursue wealth but derive pleasure from the good that they have.

I say that I read in Qoheleth bitterness, pathos, laughter, peace, like a set of transparencies.[14] Go far enough into one and it opens to the next. It is like traveling into a flower. Or like removing layers of unnecessary armor.

The Gift of God

And now a confession: I undertook this essay because I wanted to reread Ecclesiastes, a book I found bracing in youth, to see what new wisdom it might hold for me. I was certain it contained truths about life that I needed to know, advice I needed to follow and was resisting, and in fact that is the case. To learn to slide like Qoheleth from bitterness through pathos into laughter, and out into peace, would be an achievement for me. I like seeing him do it, as it were, in slow motion, intermittently and repeatedly, which is probably the best any of us can hope for.

The puzzle of God remains. I quarrel with my husband about it. He says the God of Ecclesiastes was inserted by some editor and is therefore irrelevant. I say the idea of God can never be irrelevant. He asks me, thinking to trap me, what *my* idea of God is. But I cannot be caught in that trap. I cannot claim to know what God is. Here I am a student of Qoheleth the post-modern.[15] I say that Qoheleth's representation of God is radical, not simply because his God is so impersonal, unlike the interventionist and intimate god of the covenant, the prophets and the psalms, but because the author lays contradictory images of the supreme being under our noses, as it were, and obliges us (or dares us) to recognize how irrational human worship is. Besides this, he tiptoes to the edge of asserting that God is morally unreliable.

In all his explicit statements the Witness is judiciously conservative. The injunction to "fear God" comes round on the wheel a few times. Qoheleth has "seen under the sun that in the place of judgment there is wickedness and in the place of righteousness there is wickedness," but "I said in my heart God will judge the righteous and the wicked, for there is time for every desire and every happening" (3.17). A whole section is devoted to proper behavior toward God: Walk carefully (literally "watch your step") when you go to the house of God; obedience is more acceptable than the offering of fools; watch your mouth and do not bring forth too much speech before God, for God is in heaven and you are on earth. When you make a vow to God, keep it. Better not to vow than vow and not fulfill. Don't make excuses before God, or else God may be angered by your talk and destroy the work of your hands (4.17–5.5).

If Qoheleth's God is judge and potential punisher, he is also magnanimous gift giver. A man should eat and drink and take pleasure in his work during the numbered days God has given him. "This too surely comes from the hand of God, for apart from him who eats and who enjoys? To the man who pleases him he has given wisdom and knowledge and enjoyment and to the man who displeases him he has given the task to gather and collect and give to the one who pleases God. This too is *hevel* and pursuit of *ruach*" (2.24). In 3.13 and

5.17–19, Qoheleth repeats that a man should eat and drink during the days of his life that God has given him, and that when God gives a man riches and property plus the power to enjoy them, it is God's gift; "God keeps him busy in the joy of his heart so that he will not be anxious over the days of his life," meaning probably that he won't worry about his anticipated lifespan. In 6.1–2, however, a "common evil" is that "God gives a man riches and wealth and honor but God does not give him the power to eat it but a stranger eats it." In sum, good fortune and misfortune alike are distributed by God: not a very novel view.

Qoheleth declares periodically that God has arranged everything that happens under the sun, that everything he does is inscrutable, including putting into our hearts the desire for knowledge of the universe which cannot be satisfied. "I have seen the task that God gave man to be tasked with: he makes everything beautiful in its time, but without man guessing from beginning to end, what God does" (3.10–11). The idea that God is essentially unknowable is central. The fact that men cannot guess the day of their death, cannot know what will happen in their lives or understand what happens in the world, and above all cannot know what God is doing, is a major calamity for the monkey mind of the witness, that is so engaged with trying to understand everything under the sun.

This sounds pious enough, if a bit chilly. Something is wrong with the whole picture, however. It excludes revelation. It excludes any sense of how we know what we think we know about God. If it is impossible to know anything about God's ways, then it is impossible to know that God exists, or any of the other things asserted of him—except, of course, by custom and convention. People say these things because they have always been said and are accepted as common knowledge, not because they have experienced them in the way Qoheleth asserts that he has personally tried mirth and madness, wisdom and folly, or in the way he insists that he has "seen all the oppression that is done under the sun" (4.1), has "seen that all work and skillful enterprise come from man's envy" (4.4), and so on. It follows that the fictional authority established by Qoheleth's "I," which is the authority of experience, of seeing for oneself, of *witness,* stands in conflict with the apparent authority of convention. A and not-A cancel each other. The typical modern reader tends to see the skeptical Qoheleth as real and the pious one as camouflage, or as a screen provided by a later author-editor. The reverential reader tends to accentuate the positive qualities Qoheleth attributes to God and to see the author's doubt as ultimately subsumed by faith.[16]

Rather than trying to decide which is the real Qoheleth, I like to assume that both are—in other words, that he is a walking contradiction, exactly like many of us. He believes what he has been told to believe about God's omnipotence, and he also believes that he knows nothing about it. He records these contraries without choosing between them. He may or may not be aware that they are contraries. Then again, everything he says about God might be said with eye-rolling irony. Here, too, he is like us—we postmoderns for whom reality itself is undecideable. No wonder I find him delightful, no wonder I find his God compatible. Qoheleth's God is like the dark matter and dark energy of the universe: absolutely essential to our existence but absolutely mysterious. Ninety percent of the mass of the universe, for example, is "dark matter," but we have no idea what dark matter is made of. How, then, can we suppose we know anything at all about God?

Regarding God's benevolence, the Witness hedges.[17] The lengthy passage in 5.1–7 about prudence toward God is immediately followed by an equally lengthy one about the oppression of the poor and the impermeability of bureacracy;

we are told that it is no use to complain of an official because
there is always a higher official protecting him, a higher over
that one, and the king over everyone. Is it implied that God is
just the highest in a pyramid of arbitrary powers indifferent to
justice? A little later, Qoheleth advises us in times of prosperity to enjoy the good and in adversity to remember "the one
no less than the other was God's doing" (7.14). Immediately
afterward comes an announcement that divine rewards and
punishments may not be distributed appropriately: "I have
seen all this in my *hevel* days: there is a good man who dies in
his goodness and there is a wicked man who survives in his
wickedness" (7.15). A curious passage in chapter 8, shortly after this, seems to mingle the prudence of following the king's
orders and following God's. "Since the king's word is powerful
and nobody says to him 'what are you doing,' whoever keeps a
commandment stays out of trouble" (8.2–5).

In his most fascinating and controversial set of verbal
whiplashes, Qoheleth asserts that he has seen all this and
given his heart to all that happened under the sun in a time
when man had power over man to inflict harm; and then he
saw wicked men buried in holy places and righteous men for-
gotten; also *hevel,* mist, is that the sentence for wicked deeds
is not carried out swiftly, therefore the heart of the sons of
Adam is encouraged to do evil,

> because an evil man does evil a hundred times and still
> prolongs his days; for I also know that it will be well
> with those who fear God, that they fear before him, and
> it will not be well with the wicked, neither shall he pro-
> long his days, which are as a shadow, because he does
> not fear before God. There is a *hevel* that happens in the
> world, that righteous men receive the treatment of the

evil, and evil men the treatment of the righteous. I said
this also is *hevel*. So I commended enjoyment." (8.9–15)

Supporters of a pious Qoheleth take the pious part of this quote
as the meat of the sandwich and throw away the skeptical bread
around it. Skeptics do the opposite, claiming that the pious bit
should be in scare quotes.[18] Even more confusing, though, is
how we are to take his saying (here and in many other spots)
that "this also is *hevel*." "This" may refer to the world's injustice. It may also refer to his whole internal discourse. Injustice,
justice, injustice—the mind is looping again—*this* is what's ridiculous, all this thinking and theologizing, when there is no
way on earth to know anything about God's intentions. Naturally, after catching himself in a rut like this, a man will tell
himself to eat, drink, and be merry. Naturally, too, as soon
as he does so, he flips back into remembering that "there is
one event to the righteous and to the evil, to the good and
the clean and to the unclean, to one who sacrifices and one
who does not sacrifice. As is the good, so is the wicked, and
the swearer as one who fears swearing . . . one event to all"
(9.2–3), which is death, and nobody knows when death will
arrive. From Qoheleth it is but one step to Job, and another
step to Kafka.

He never takes the step. As often as he arrives at the
moral desert, he asserts that it is actually a garden. "I" comes
eyeball to eyeball with the looking glass and passes through
to the other side. The transience of all mortal phenomena
opens like a morning flower. God is the name we give to the
force that through the green fuse drives the flower, and also
kills it. That is all we actually know about God, and to know
how little we know should, after the frustration quiets down,
make us happy. "Death is the mother of beauty," says Wallace

Stevens. In Ecclesiastes, failure and death are the mother and father of happiness. We can stop thinking about the fruit of action. We can be here now.

The point becomes clear that there is no point and that the process of recognizing the pointlessness of life, of our own lives, is a struggle like fighting one's way through a wind tunnel. The wind of the spirit blows always downstream while we struggle upstream thinking surely we can make it to the other side where all will be clarified and serene under the sun, until we surrender in exhaustion and the wind then carries us where it will. For some of us this will happen only at the moment of death. But a living dog is better than a dead lion. "One is obliged to bless for the evil as well as for the good," says the Mishnah (Berachot 9.5). Some of us will choose life and try to live it.

One may wonder how Ecclesiastes made its way into the Bible. Curiously, although Talmud (Tractate Sabbath 306) records that "the sages wished to hide the book of Ecclesiastes" (i.e., exclude it from the canon), the reason was not what we might think—the author's denial that God gives meaning to life—but rather the author's advice to youth to "walk in the ways of your heart," which was considered dangerous. The school of Shammai opposed canonization while its rival, the school of Hillel, supported it; the latter won. Of the book as a whole, Talmud continues, "its beginning is religious and its end is religious." So far as I am concerned, the spirituality of Ecclesiastes consists less in its final advice to fear God and keep the commandments—a line presumably added to make the book more respectable—than in its vivid articulation of the conviction that existence is God's mystery, that life is God's gift, and that "God" is the name for everything I cannot understand.

JONAH:
THE BOOK OF THE QUESTION

If we obey God, we must disobey ourselves.
—HERMAN MELVILLE,
MOBY DICK

A nd the Lord prepared a great fish to swallow up Jonah; and Jonah was in the belly of the fish three days and three nights. . . . And the Lord spoke unto the fish, and it vomited Jonah out upon the dry land." Children love it. Very young ones listen very carefully. Older ones are inclined to remark "yuck," or perhaps "cool." Jonah-and-the-whale is what most people remember of the story, and it has the same sort of childish appeal as Noah's ark, another sensational yarn involving storm and survival, death-threat and enclosure.

There is more to it than that. Each year on Yom Kippur, the Day of Atonement, which is the most solemn in the Jewish calendar, the Book of Jonah is read in the afternoon service, *minhah.* Here, it is a parable about repentance, emphasizing the idea of a universally merciful God, but told in such a folk-tale style that it usually functions as a bit of relief from the weightiness of the day—at least, until the last sentence.

The last sentence of the Book of Jonah impels us into outer space. Or perhaps it is inner space. The whole book has led us into the web of what T. S. Eliot calls an "overwhelming question." In this most politically and psychologically fraught tale, inner and outer space, the world and the self, become dark mirrors to each other.

The story consists of four brief chapters, each a clear unit, each unit taking a hairpin turn from what comes before.

Running Away

When God calls you, you have some options. You can say, "Here am I," like Abraham. You can be present, your soul an open book; you can make yourself fearlessly receptive and ready to be entered. Or you can try to hide like Adam, when God comes looking for you in the garden in the cool of the day, because you are ashamed of being naked. You can try to resist whatever it is God wants of you. Why me? says Moses, who has to be elaborately convinced that he can speak to Pharaoh despite his speech impediment (Exodus 3.4–10). Prophets commonly protest their incapacity when first confronted by divine command. Jeremiah fears that he is like a child who "does not know how to speak" (Jeremiah 1.6). Isaiah insists, "I am a man of unclean lips" (Isaiah 6.5). In a way, the initial self-doubt of a holy man may be a sign of his holiness.

Or you can run. Most of us run. We are busy people, we have a hundred things to accomplish every day, endless obligations to keep us running, too busy for anything like a still small voice—which might be God's voice, might be our own—we really don't want to hear. A plane to catch, the cleaning to pick up, the papers to plow through, the car to get repaired, the dishes to wash, the calls to make. The kids to ferry, the dinner, the doctor, the vacation, the theater tickets. The beer to drink, the pills to take. Possibly we sense a cold wind at our backs, the whir of wheels, but if we keep moving, whatever it is won't catch up. If we keep the internal volume raised, with all its useful cacophonous static, we may manage never to hear that commanding voice.

Jonah is somebody who wishes he never heard it. In 2 Kings 14.25, a "Jonah son of Ammitai" is called a prophet and is said to have lived in the time of King Jereboam, in the eighth century BCE. The apocryphal book of Tobit (14.4, 8) also refers to a prophet Jonah. But the Jonah of the book of Jonah is never called a prophet. An ordinary man, he does what most of us might do. His tale is packed with amazing events that are fiction-candy to children and grownups, but instead of Odysseus or Superman, it has an anti-hero at its narrative center.

Jonah runs. He hears one sentence and he flies. His name means "dove," which in Torah usually suggests good and auspicious things. A dove finds land for Noah (Genesis 8.11–12). In an image of salvation in Psalm 68.14, "The wings of the dove are covered with silver, and her pinions with the shimmer of gold." In Song of Songs 5.2, it becomes an endearment: "my dove, my perfect one." The Zohar, however, treats Jonah's name as a participle of *ynh,* to oppress or maltreat, and calls him "the aggrieved one." [1] Jonah, however, is far from perfect. Whether he is to be seen as aggrieved or oppressed is for the reader to decide.

The sentence Jonah has heard is "Arise [or, more colloquially, Get up], go to Nineveh, that great city, and cry out against it, for their wickedness has come up before me" (1.2). The situation parallels what happens in other prophetic books, with one major difference. Jonah is being asked to preach to pagans. Nineveh is a huge Assyrian city famous for evil-doing and violence, which might lead us to expect a Sodom and Gomorrah plotline. But Jonah wants no part of this plot. He "arose to flee to Tarshish from the presence of the Lord. He

went down to Joppa, and found a ship going to Tarshish; so
he paid the fare, and went down into it, to go with them to
Tarshish from the presence of the Lord" (1.3). This is maxi-
mally speedy storytelling, which leaves us no time to ask
what Jonah's reasons are. The story lets us feel that he doesn't
have reasons, doesn't need reasons, just acts on instinct—the
instinct to escape. Joppa, the modern Jaffa south of today's
Tel Aviv, has been a port city for thousands of years. Scholars
have never actually located Tarshish, but the point of it seems
to be that Tarshish is in exactly the opposite direction from
Nineveh, effectively at the ends of the earth, perhaps some-
where in Spain, perhaps Cadiz. It is said that Tarshish was beyond the area of the world where Jahweh's name was known.
Jonah might be thinking that if the people in Tarshish have
never heard of God, perhaps God won't find him there, perhaps "the presence of God" doesn't reach that far. Of course,
we as audience are expected to know better, and to recognize
in advance that Jonah is fooling himself. Story logic in every
culture says that we can run but we can't hide. God's universal presence is sung in Psalm 139, a psalm affirming God's
absolute knowledge of all the singer's ways and words, even in
the womb, and the impossibility of hiding anything from his
omniscience and omnipresence:

> Whither shall I go from thy spirit?
> Or whither shall I flee from thy presence?
> If I ascend up into heaven, thou art there,
> If I make my bed in hell, behold, thou art there.
> If I take the wings of the morning,
> And dwell in the uttermost parts of the sea,
> Even there shall thy hand lead me,
> And thy right hand shall hold me. (7–10)

Still, we can recognize Jonah's impulse in ourselves. It is an irrational impulse, perhaps, like that of a child who hopes to escape a parental demand, but no less universal for being irrational. The desire to escape destiny goes at least as far back as the Oedipus story. The drive to flee social and religious constraint is poignantly explored in American literature, these thousands of years later, from Melville's Ishmael and Twain's Huck Finn to Gatsby, Kerouac, and beyond.

But the action in the Jonah story is swift. Jonah tries to escape, "But the Lord hurled a great wind into the sea, and there was a mighty tempest in the sea, so that the ship was like to be broken" (1.4). The sailors are afraid, pray to their gods and cast their freight overboard, while Jonah, fast asleep in the bottom of the ship, has to be wakened by the captain who urges him to pray: "Get up," cries the captain, using the same imperative as God, "call upon your god, it may be that the god will think upon us, that we perish not" (1.6). Notice that the term here is the generic elohim, not Jahweh. The crew casts lots to see who is to blame for the storm, and, when the lot falls on Jonah and they ask him who is, he replies, "I am a Hebrew; and I fear the Lord, the God of heaven, who has made the sea and the dry land" (1.9). Notice that Jonah does use the name Jahweh here. Now the sailors are "very afraid," and Jonah tells them to throw him overboard to stop the storm. Instead, they row harder, but the storm grows worse. Beseeching the Lord not to hold them guilty of innocent blood, they throw Jonah overboard. The storm stops immediately. The sailors then "feared the Lord exceedingly; and they offered a sacrifice unto the Lord, and they made vows" (1.16).

This closes Jonah's opening chapter. The chapter has given us a sense of God's universal power in the cosmos and over nature, as well as evidence that Jonah is well aware of that power. It has also given us our first picture of virtuous pagans, for the behavior of the crew is morally exemplary. A charming midrash in the ninth-century *Pirke Eleazer* says that men of all seventy languages on earth were on board and that they dipped Jonah into the raging ocean three times— first to his knees, then his navel, then his neck, the storm abating each time but beginning again when they lifted him—before they reluctantly decided to cast him overboard.[2] Most hauntingly, the chapter gives us a Jonah whose impulse to escape is as powerful as God's determination to prevent his escape. There are hints that what he wants to escape is not simply God, but himself. Jonah goes "down" to Joppa, "down" into the ship, "down into the bowels of the ship" where his stupor during the tempest implies a quest for oblivion. When he finally volunteers, it is not to pray like the ship's crew, or to do what God has required, but to be drowned.

The Fish

Chapter two begins with the fish swallowing Jonah. Here it seems we are at the heart of the fable, or rather the belly of the beast—at any rate, its most familiar symbol. Are we terrified, are we relieved? Surely both. I remember from adolescence a deliciously frightening comic book character called The Heap, who rose from slime and engulfed enemies. Before that, I applauded when the crocodile got Captain Hook. From *The Little Shop of Horrors* to *Jaws* and beyond, a fleet of film fantasies involves organisms with monstrous swallowing capacities. At the same time, our fear of being engulfed, our terror of the devouring mother, our fear of the dissolution of self is, perhaps like all fears, mingled with desire. Like Keats, Jonah seems "half in love with easeful death"; in fact, as numerous commentators have observed, what we see in Jonah from the outset looks very like a latent death-wish. To be sucked into a belly that is reassuring womb as well as terrifying tomb means the cessation of anxiety. In other words, the fish is the completely appropriate solution to Jonah's wish to escape, in which punishment for guilt blends with gratifying regression.

It is also a playground for interpreters. In *Pirke Eleazer,* the fish's belly is like a great synagogue, with eyes for windows and a huge pearl hanging from the ceiling to give light; the fish takes Jonah on a suboceanic tour in exchange for being saved from Leviathan, an even bigger fish. *Midrash Jonah,* in response to a feminine ending on the fish in 2.1 (*ha-dagah* instead of *ha-dag* in 1.17) has him spat out by the initial fish into the mouth of a "pregnant fish with 365,000 small fish in her" whom God has appointed in order to make Jonah more uncomfortable. Condemning Jonah as being like a wet nurse who refuses to suckle the king's own son, the midrash describes his skin as being eaten away by fishy digestive juices so that he finally yields to God "the prayer of the righteous." Both these treatments have a distinctly humorous touch. The Zohar, however, sees Jonah's descent as the soul's descent into the world at birth—"Man, then, is in this world as in a ship that is traversing the great ocean and is like to be broken"[3] —and sees the fish story as an allegory of death and resurrection. So, too, in a different way, Matthew 12.30: "As Jonah was in the belly of the sea monster three days and three nights, so will the Son of Man be in the heart of the earth three days and three nights." For the early Christian Fathers, Jonah is a prototype of Jesus, although in later Christian interpretation he becomes an emblem of Jewish stubbornness. The author of the Middle English poem "Patience" gives a splendidly elaborate picture of Jonah's sojourn "in fat and in filth . . . nothing

but muck and mire." In Father Mapple's sermon in *Moby Dick,*
Jonah is a contemptible and tormented criminal grateful for
his punishment, while by the end of the novel the whale and
God are indistinguishably fused.

Twentieth-century interpretations of the fish belly also
vary widely. For Carl Jung the fish illustrates the principle
that "only in the region of danger (watery abyss, cavern, for-
west, island, castle, etc.)," can one find "the treasure hard to
attain (jewel, virgin, life-potion, victory over death)."[4] In the
poet Stephen Mitchell's "Jonah," the fish resembles an ana-
lyst's comfortable couch. In Wolf Mankiewitz's one-act play
It Should Happen to a Dog, Jonah delivers quips like a standup
Yiddish-inflected comedian, and the fish-belly smells like
Billingsgate (the East London fish market). Norma Rosen's
"Justice for Jonah, or a Bible Bartleby," gives Jonah a vision
of future Jewish suffering down to the Holocaust as a correc-
tive to the idea of a God of justice. For George Orwell in the
essay "Inside the Whale," the belly represents irresponsible
apolitical quietism that accepts "concentration camps, rubber
truncheons, Hitler, Stalin, bombs . . . putsches, purges." And
novelist Julian Barnes, with another political slant, describes
Jonah's God as a fascist dictator, western imperialist, or moralistic bully.[5]

It is important to notice that just as chapter 1 of Jonah
spends no time analyzing Jonah's motives, so chapter 2 dwells
not at all on the fish's symbolism—which is probably why
Jonah's readers have been encouraged to be so fertile with interpretations. The unsaid draws us to fill in the blanks with
our own myths and fantasies. In fact, chapter 2 takes just two
sentences to say that Jonah was swallowed by the fish, was in
the fish's belly three days and three nights, and then prayed.
The entire remainder of chapter 2 is the text of Jonah's prayer,
followed by the Lord's instruction to the fish to spew him out.

With the prayer we go abruptly from prose to poetry, and from efficiently zippy narrative to sublimity. The text reads like a collage of lines from a variety of psalms, with emphasis on descent, watery submersion, and salvation:

> Out of my affliction I called to the Lord, and he an-
>   swered me;
> Out of the belly of Sheol I cried, and you heard my
>   voice.
> For you did cast me into the deep, into the heart of the
>   seas,
> So that your floods surrounded me, all your billows and
>   waves passed over me.
> Then I said, I have been cast out from your sight, yet
>   will I look again to your holy temple.
> The waters surrounded me, even to my soul; the deep
>   closed around me.
> Weeds were wrapped around my head; I went down to
>   the bottoms of the mountains; the earth with her
>   bars closed upon me for ever.
> Yet you have brought my life up from the pit, O Lord
>   my God.
> When my soul fainted within me, I remembered the
>   Lord,
> And my prayer went up to you, into your holy temple.
> Those who regard worthless idols forsake their own
>   mercy.
> But I will sacrifice to you with the voice of thanksgiving:
> I will fulfill what I have vowed. Deliverance belongs to
>   the Lord. (Jonah 2.2–9)

There are some odd things about this prayer, despite its powerful imagery. First, it seems to be expressing gratitude for something that has not yet happened. Jonah has not actually been rescued, although he talks as if he had. Is he hoping to move the Lord proleptically? Is he simply scavenging for appropriate phrases? Is he perhaps grateful to be where he is? Second, notwithstanding its beautiful metaphor, Jonah's prayer does not, in fact, express repentance for disobedience. It imagines and vows temple worship and sacrifice, rituals unconnected with God's original command to him. The astute reader may recall the numerous occasions in prophetic literature when God insists that he despises mere ritual worship unaccompanied by deeds of justice. However, when the prayer is followed by Jonah's deliverance back to dry land, it appears that God has found it acceptable. At this point, we may think we have a rather conventional death-and-rebirth story. We must think again.

Nineveh Repents

At the opening of chapter 3, God hits the repeat button: "And the word of the Lord came to Jonah the second time, saying, Get up, go to Nineveh, that great city, and proclaim to it the message that I tell you" (3.1). We are firmly if rather humorously back exactly where we started. This time Jonah goes, "according to the word of the Lord" (3.3). What follows has, just as much as the whale tale, the quality of fantasy and hyperbole. We are told that Nineveh "was an exceedingly great city" (*ir ha-gadol l'elohim*), literally a great city to God, or as we might put it, a Godawful great city, of "three days' journey" (3.3). At its height, judging by its archeological remains, Nineveh would have taken an hour or so to traverse, but the story needs exaggeration. Marvelously exaggerated too is the Ninevite response to Jonah's arrival. "Jonah began to enter the city a day's journey, and he proclaimed, and said, 'Forty more days and Nineveh shall be overthrown'" (3.4), at which the Ninevites immediately believe God, start to fast, and put on sackcloth "from the greatest to the least" (3.5). When the king hears of this he too dons sackcloth, rises from his throne and sits in the dust, orders fasting and sackcloth not only for people but for animals: "Let neither man nor beast, herd nor flock, taste any thing; let them not feed, nor drink water, but let them be covered with sackcloth, both man and beast, and let them cry mightily unto God." Moreover, he adds, "let them turn every one from his evil way, and from the violence that is in their hands. Who knows if God will not turn away from his hot anger, that we perish not?" (3.7–8)

So here is the second instance, far more wonderful and improbable than the first, of righteous pagans. Trying to imagine cows mooing mightily to God is funny.[6] But the idea that the conversion happens from the ground up—populace first, king afterward—is important, as is the idea that repentance consists not only in ritual acts but in ceasing from evil and violence. Significantly, the king of Nineveh understands that the propitiation of a deity may or may not be successful. His "who knows," like the "may be" of the captain, underscores the mystery of divine will. The "God" to which both he and his people refer is not the Jahweh of the Hebrews but the more generic (and plural form) "Elohim." Yet in his hope that when people "turn," God too may "turn," he duplicates precisely the theology of Atonement essential to Yom Kippur, as well as the language of many Hebrew prophets who, in God's name, promise precisely this to the straying children of Israel. If they turn, he will turn. If they repent, so will he. So it turns out. "And God saw their works, that they repented from their evil way, and God repented of the evil which he said he would do unto them, and he did it not" (3.10). "Forty more days and Nineveh will be overthrown" has, incidentally, a double meaning. *Hafak,* overthrow or overturn, is the word used for what happens to Sodom and Gomorrah (Genesis 19.29, Deuteronomy 30.23, Amos 4.11, Jeremiah 20.16, Lamentations 4.6). However, as with oracles in classical Greece, which can mean the opposite of what they seem (in the most famous instance an oracle tells the Lydian king Croesus that if he attacks Persia a great kingdom will be overthrown, but neglects to tell him it will be his own kingdom), *hafak* can also mean to turn over or turn around. Jonah presumably did not think of that.

At this point, it looks as if the didactic thrust of the story is that non-Israelites are subject not only to God's wrath, but also to God's mercy. The greatness of God is to be understood as universal and absolute, the will of God is to be understood as free.[7] In a core statement of his readiness to change his mind, God announces to the prophet Jeremiah:

> At one instant I may speak concerning a kingdom, to pluck up and to break down and destroy it, but if that nation turn from their evil, because of which I have spoken against it, I repent of the evil that I thought to do to it. And at one instant I may speak concerning a nation, and concerning a kingdom, to build and to plant it; but if it do evil in my sight, that it hearken not to my voice, then I repent of the good, wherewith I said I would benefit it. (Jeremiah 18.7–10)

The Jonah story is also implicitly proposing that pagans can be more deserving of God's mercy than Israelites. When God charges Jeremiah to go to King Jehokiam, saying "It may be that the house of Judah will hear all the evil which I purpose to do to them, that they may return every man from

their evil way, and I may forgive their iniquity and their sin"
(Jeremiah 36.3), the king cuts the prophet's scroll in two and
throws it into the fire; as a consequence, "man and beast"
will suffer disaster (Jeremiah 36.29). The king of Nineveh
is clearly intended as a contrast to King Jehokiam. Surely if
Nineveh can so successfully repent, it can be a model for Israel? If a pagan city can turn from the injustice and violence
in its midst, cannot Israel do the same? "As I live, says the
Lord, I have no pleasure in the death of the wicked, but that
the wicked turn from his way and live" (Ezekiel 33.11).

In this context we need to notice that after Jonah's initial
pronouncement, he disappears from the vast collective action
of chapter 3. We understand that his proclamation has pre-
cipitated all this action, but the Ninevites believe "God" (Elohim) rather than Jonah; although he has been the center of the
story until now, in chapter 3 he shrinks to vanishing point.
This diminution will be essential to the scenario of chapter 4.

Sitting in the Desert

The opening of chapter 4 is stunning in its surprise and its
force. The Ninevites have repented, and so has God; "he did
it not." Everyone has survived. We do not actually know if
hafak is the word God dictated to Jonah or if he chose it himself, but either way, we can imagine God sitting back, deeply
pleased at the outcome. We might consider this the happy
ending we have been waiting for and which the descent-and-
re-ascent theme anticipated,[8] but we would be wrong. On the
heels of "he did it not" comes this:

> And it displeased Jonah exceedingly, and he was angry.
> And he prayed to the Lord, and said, O Lord, was not

this what I said, when I was still in my own country? Therefore I fled before to Tarshish. For I knew that you are a gracious God, and merciful, slow to anger, and abundant in lovingkindness, and who relents from doing evil. Therefore now, I beseech you Lord, take my life from me; for it is better for me to die than live. (4.1–3)

God responds to this in a question that may be translated as "Are you greatly angry?" or "Is it good for you to be angry?"

The issue is the fate of nations. The question could not be starker. Some traditional Jewish interpretations, as well as some modern commentators, claim that Jonah is angry that God has made a liar of him; he fears he will be condemned as a "false prophet." Others say Jonah fears that Ninevite repentance will cause God's wrath to turn against a recalcitrant Israel. Still others argue that he wants to avoid saving a people who will later be among Israel's cruelest enemies. The Assyrian empire of which Nineveh was the capital conquered the northern kingdom of Israel in 721 BCE and drove its surviving inhabitants into exile. In one midrash, Ninevite repentance lasted only forty days.[9]

But Jonah's declaration that foreknowledge of God's mercy was what caused him to flee to Tarshish need not be taken at face value. On the contrary, we seem to be looking at a classical instance of passive aggression. "And it was evil to Jonah a great evil and it burned to him" is the literal translation of 4.1. The word for the evil, *ha-ra'ah,* may indicate wickedness, distress, or harm; the same ambiguous word is used for the evil of the Ninevites before their repentance and for the evil God planned to do to them before his own repentance. God has turned from the heat of his anger (3.9), and now Jonah is burning up with it. His barely controlled rage at the idea that

Nineveh will not be destroyed is as dramatic as any of the story's more sensational happenings. Here the comic elements in the story turn dark, as the veiled hints of pathology in Jonah's character abruptly intensify. Jonah has sought to escape not only God's command, God's regime, but the light of day. As Jonathan Magonet puts it, "Jonah in flight is on a journey away from God, on a journey towards death." [10] He has got himself below the waterline of his ship and slept like a dead man through the tempest. The belly of the fish was somehow where he wanted to be. Forcibly vomited forth, he has done what he had to do. His preaching has been effective beyond any prophet's wildest dreams. Now, exposed to the brightness of the desert sun, he is like an angry shadow.

In *The Brothers Karamazov,* Ivan asks Alyosha if he would, given the ability to do so, make the world into a paradise for human beings, at the cost of one child being beaten for eternity. Alyosha does not speak for a long time and finally, weeping, says "No."

Alyosha does not command a mass audience. As we know from a century of genocide that has touched every continent on the planet, the ease with which human beings can contemplate, not to mention participate in, the elimination of whole categories of fellow-creatures, seems to be rather basic to our species. People can be converted to wishing death to Americans, or Armenians, or Blacks, or Jews, or Palestinians, or Croatians, or Hutus, or homosexuals, or anyone who wears glasses and can read; and they can be furiously indignant if prevented. We have in the United States the phenomenon of "shock jocks," radio talk show hosts who imitate the manners of the sort of adolescent boy who has discovered he can get attention by being loudly, crudely, publicly bad. One such entertainer is famous for saying "There is only one way to get rid of nuclear weapons—use them." Another called on the president to "drop a nuclear weapon" on a random Arab capital: "I think these people need to be forcibly converted to Christianity," he told his many millions of listeners. "It's the only thing that can probably turn them into human beings." The gleeful stupidity of such utterances may be feigned for commercial purposes, but the hostility they represent is surely real, and addresses a welcoming audience.

Now let us imagine Jonah, utterly alone, sun beating down on him, praying to God to take his life. Of course he *knew* (or claims he did) that God was gracious and merciful, and so on. Everyone knows that. These words are central to Jewish liturgy because they are the words with which God proclaims his own attributes to Moses on Sinai: "Now the Lord descended in the cloud and stood with him there and proclaimed, The Lord, the Lord God, gracious and merciful, longsuffering and abounding in lovingkindness and truth, keeping mercy to the thousandth generation, forgiving iniquity and transgression and sin" (Exodus 34.5–7).[11] But Jonah, like many of us—Jews, Christians, Muslims—*does not in fact want God to be merciful.* Jonah speaks the familiar devotional words with bitter teeth-grinding irony. It is as if he were saying to God, "I knew you would act like a frigging bleeding-heart liberal." He would rather die than see the Ninevites unharmed and himself embarrassed after predicting their annihilation. Here is one of the most devastating insights in the entire Bible. When God asks him if he is right to be so angry, Jonah does not answer. Does not deign to answer. Cannot. Too sullen to speak, he leaves the city and sits on its east side, making himself a shelter and waiting to see what will happen to the city. He wants it to suffer the fate of Sodom and Gomorrah, apparently. Cataclysmic fire, smoke, and ashes are what he waits for. He wants to see God nuke the city.

Just as he earlier appointed a fish, God at this point appoints a gourd to grow up over Jonah to give him shade and deliver him from misery. Jonah is "exceedingly grateful" for the gourd, in a mood swing that mirrors how he was "exceedingly angry" a short while before, for he is unaware that God now is playing a game with him. At dawn God appoints a worm to attack the plant so that it withers. When the sun rises he appoints a scorching east wind. Imagine Jonah now sitting there in the desert, fainting in the heat that reflects his own anger (just as the storm reflects his own storm) but also the desert sun, and thrashed by the east wind that is also the soul, *ruach*. "It is better for me to die than to live," he says. Now comes God's delicate joke. God has set Jonah up with the gourd trick.

> And God said to Jonah, Is it right for you to be angry about the gourd? And he said, I do right to be angry, even unto death. Then said the Lord, You pity the gourd for which you have not labored nor made it grow, which was born in a night and perished in a night. And should I not pity Nineveh, that great city, in which are more than a hundred and twenty thousand persons who do not know their right hand from their left, and also much cattle? (Jonah 4.9–11)

Curtain. Blackout. The Book of Jonah concludes with this unanswered question. To read it is like running at top speed into a glass wall. Of course, God knows quite well that Jonah does not pity the plant, only himself. Pretending that he thinks otherwise is merely a tease, the divine tongue in the divine cheek. His description of the Ninevites as simple innocents is breathtakingly different from describing them either as wicked or as repentant; it is rather a means of making clear that from God's perspective they are mere human beings, pathetic creatures not terribly different from their cattle. The cattle seem to be the crowning absurd touch in God's little joke. Or perhaps this punch line is more than a joke, more than a way of equating the Ninevites with dumb animals, and even more than a statement of God's ecological sensitivities. Cattle are supposed to rest on Shabbat just as people are. Chillingly, the twentieth century's most powerful single image of the disasters of war may be the screaming horse at the center of Picasso's *Guernica*.

The silence at the end of the book of Jonah is one of the most remarkable silences in all of literature. In both the Masoretic Torah and the Dead Sea Scrolls a space is left in the text after Jonah's statement that he wants to die. The space indicates that Jonah's shocking utterance must give us pause. Now at the text's final stopping place, the silent space expands to circle the globe. *Should I not pity Nineveh, that great city, in which are more than one hundred and twenty thousand persons who cannot tell their right hand from their left, and also much cattle?* The question hangs in the air. The air is filled with ghosts. The silence in the air is as resonant as the final sentence of Beckett's *The Unnameable:* "I can't go on, I'll go on." [12]

It is like the silence at the end of Dan Pagis's poem, "Written in Pencil in a Sealed Railway Car":

> here in this transport
> I eve
> and abel my son
> if you should see my older son
> cain son of man
>
> tell him that I

Jonah as Everyman

The stories of the prophets are peculiar to Jewish history. These men lived and preached in a tiny, rocky land that to them was a land of milk and honey, and in a city in which stood one of the greatest temples of the then-known world. They attacked corrupt kings; they attacked corrupt priests; they attacked the rich and powerful of their own society; they predicted the downfall of their own nation. In God's name— commanded by God—they raved in the street, saying what God ordered them to say. Feed widows, children and strangers. Do justice, love mercy. Don't take bribes. Pay workers the wages you've promised. Worship the true God, not idols. All of this was too difficult for the Israelites.

It is still too difficult for us. God was raving at the Israelites through the voices of the prophets. The audience could not hear, of course, just as we cannot. As a consequence, the prophets often experience abuse, death threats, despair. Still, it is to the prophetic tradition that we owe the concept of free speech, of "speaking truth to power," as well as the concept of social justice.

Jonah is not a typical prophet, though he is given that title in Kings. Jonah seems to be the underside of prophecy, the seams and hanging threads of righteousness. The uprooted tree shows its massive system of roots with earthen clods still clinging to them. Perhaps Jonah is a parody prophet. Perhaps he is intended as the model bad example in contrast to Isaiah, Ezekiel, Jeremiah, and the rest. But Jonah is also Everyman.[13] He is our stubborn fear of change, our rejection of connection and love, our secret death wish. His is the despair, the depression, that is a kind of paralysis in human life. The story of

Jonah connects the psychic dots that demonstrate the link between self-hatred and hatred of others. To put that link theologically, we might say Jonah sits sullenly in that place within each of us that resists doing what we know God wants.

And what does the God who made heaven and earth want of us now, each in our little sphere of existence? Do we have a clue? Do we have any idea what God wants us to do collectively, as nations? Does anyone even think to ask? Those who are confident that they already know are legion. The worst, as Yeats said, are full of passionate intensity. The best lack all conviction. Nobody has ears to hear. If I were God, I would be upset. I would feel like a betrayed lover, which is a figure that recurs all through prophetic literature. Or, more likely, I would feel like a teacher in an unruly classroom.

God is patient with Jonah as one would be with a child who needs to learn a lesson. When Jonah runs from God, God hurls a storm at him. When he tries to die, God saves him, sets him on his feet and repeats the original instruction. When he sulks, God steps back and asks him to look at himself. When he goes on sulking, God teases him. Their final conversation is worthy of first place in any collection of aggressive jokes. Freud comments on "the situation in which one person adopts a humorous attitude toward others": "the subject is behaving towards them as an adult towards a child when he recognizes and smiles at the triviality of interests and sufferings which seem so great to it. Thus the humorist would acquire his superiority by assuming the role of the grown-up . . . and reducing others to being children."[14] But perhaps God merely wants Jonah and the rest of us to *grow up*. Perhaps the strategy of telling Jonah's story like a child's story is designed to put us in touch with how much of the sulking child we each retain.

Grow up? Well, we won't if we don't want to. We'd rather die.

And so we leave the Jonah who is an aspect of ourselves sitting in the desert outside Nineveh, a desert we may imagine as resembling that of Los Alamos, where the first nuclear weapon was developed. The actual Nineveh was destroyed in the year 612 BCE; but it was never a place merely of myth. Its site was across the Tigris River from the present-day city of Mosul, in present-day Iraq. Here too we leave God with his unanswered question of whether we human beings (Jonah in the first instance, Israelites in the second, but of course the book is written for *everyone*) should prefer to see Others, who share the planet with us, creatures who do not know their right hand from their left, and also much cattle, destroyed or saved.

⚜

JOB:
THE OPEN BOOK

Thou art indeed just, Lord, if I contend

With thee; but, Sir, so what I plead is just.

Why do sinners' ways prosper? And why must

Disappointment all I endeavor end?

—GERARD MANLY HOPKINS,
"THOU ART INDEED JUST"

I t is one of the oldest questions in the world. Every bright kid who hears that God is supposed to be all-powerful, all-knowing, and all-good, asks it, and every religion somehow must deal with it. Why do bad things happen to good people? Why is there suffering and death? Why did God let my dog die, the child might ask. Later, the child might ask: Why the holocaust? Why genocide?

Of all the countertexts in the Bible, the Book of Job is the most forthrightly provocative. Addressing the traditional idea that God always rewards the good and punishes the guilty, the Book of Job reminds us in magnificent language of what we actually fear but do not like to say: God does no such thing. Far more than Ecclesiastes, who hints at the amorality of the divine will but does not press the point, the author of the Book of Job mounts a stunning, ferocious, and sublime indictment of God's justice. We are given the portrait of a perfectly good and faithful man whom God decides to torture. We see that man in anguish, in rage, cursing the day of his birth, wishing to die, wishing that he had never been born. We see his wife telling him to curse God and die. We see his pious friends exacerbating his suffering by insisting that he must have sinned in order to deserve it—blaming the victim, as this righteous activity would be called today. We see him insisting, rightly, on his innocence, begging for an explanation of his suffering, calling God to account, demanding that God respond to him. And God does respond. In fact, God responds twice. For there are, in fact, *two* endings to the Book of Job—and it looks as if God contradicts himself. Can this be, and if so, what might that mean for us?

Job is a thought experiment of an extremely complicated and unusual sort, because it sets a problem and does *not* offer a solution. Instead, it gives us something like a Zen koan, designed to crack our reasoning minds open.

Torah: What's Justice Got to Do With It

It is a strange obsession of the children of God, God's justice. That a god should be just, obliged to reward good men who obeyed his laws, cared for widows and the poor and so forth, and punish evil ones who did not, was not a notion crucial to Egyptian, Canaanite, or Babylonian religions. In the Babylonian epic *Gilgamesh,* the gods have created human beings essentially to be their slaves. The Greek gods with whom we are familiar from Homer are notoriously a quarrelsome and lascivious lot who pick sides in human wars for purely narcissistic reasons.[1] We should appreciate, if we step back from our theological assumptions, how peculiar an expectation it is that human justice should be intrinsic to a god. It is still more odd that human beings should need to remind the god about this. Yet such is the case time and again in the Bible.

When God confides to Abraham that he is about to destroy the city of Sodom, the appalled Abraham asks, "Wilt thou also destroy the righteous with the wicked? Peradventure there be fifty righteous within the city. . . . Shall not the Judge of all the earth do right?" (Genesis 18.23–25). In the scene that follows, Abraham bargains with God, who ultimately agrees not to destroy the city if even ten good people are found in it. Of course, we soon learn that the ten are not found, and Sodom is destroyed; yet how fascinating that God indulges Abraham in a bargaining session. In this scene we see the origin of Jewish *chutzpah.* Jacob's wrestling with the angel (Genesis 32.24–32) and Jeremiah's outcry "Wherefore doth the way of the wicked prosper" (Jeremiah 12.1) set man against God in two different ways, one heroic, one anguished. In a striking scene in the Exodus story, Moses prevents a wrathful God from destroying the Israelites after they have worshiped the Golden Calf, by reminding him of his promises to Abraham, Isaac, and Jacob, and pointing out that the Egyptians will think him crazy if he destroys his own people: "And God repented of the evil which he thought to do" (Exodus 32.7–14). This is gambling for high stakes indeed, and God does not agree to forgive; in fact, he vows to blot out "whosoever hath sinned against me," but Moses himself remains unpunished. In Psalm 89, King David both remembers that God has made an explicit covenant with him and that he seems to have broken it: "How long, lord? Wilt thou hide thyself for ever? Shall thy wrath burn like fire? . . . where are thy former lovingkindnesses, which thou swearest unto David in thy truth?" (Psalms 89.46–49). None of these bold heroes, however, goes as far as Job does.

The Prose Frame

In the folktale frame to the story of Job, from whose center sublime poetry will explode, the tone is matter of fact. It is business as usual, and it is in prose, which might remind us of how Shakespeare in his tragedies liked to include earthy scenes in prose. God and Satan converse one day in heaven:

> And the Lord said to Satan, Have you considered my servant Job, that there is none like him in the earth, a blameless and upright man, one that fears God and shuns evil? (1.8)

We might hear a bit of a boast here—or a bit of relief that at least *one* human being is doing the right thing, or perhaps God is simply impressed at how good this one man is. Satan remarks that Job has never been tested by suffering, and we have already been told how extremely wealthy Job is—"the greatest of all the men of the east" (1.3)—so God gives Satan permission to afflict him, in order to see if Job will curse his maker as Satan claims. It is important to remember here that "Satan" is not the fiend he becomes in Christian lore. He is one of the "sons of God," an angel who is part courtier, part spy, and who has just the powers God gives him.[2] Job's cattle are immediately stolen or slain, his servants killed, and his seven sons and three daughters die when a great wind destroys the house in which they are gathered. To this Job's response is a wholly yielding one; he rends his clothes, falls down, and worships: "Naked came I out of my mother's womb, and naked shall I return there: the Lord gave, and the Lord has taken away; blessed be the name of the Lord." God seems to have won the wager and boasts in a second interview, "Have you considered my servant Job . . . still he holds fast to his integrity, although you incited me against him, to destroy him without cause" (2.3). But Satan ups the ante by claiming that if Job is physically afflicted he will then curse God. God agrees to let Satan do as he wishes, and Job's body is afflicted with unbearable boils. Again Job submits, rebuking the wife who tells him to curse God and die. "Shall we receive good at the hand of God," he declares, "and shall we not receive evil?" When three friends arrive to mourn and comfort him, they hardly recognize him as he sits on his ash heap scraping his body with a potsherd.

The modern reader may be puzzled: Why does God give Satan all this power? Why does he let himself be needled by one of his own servants? Is he that insecure? Should we, as Carl Jung suggests in "An Answer to Job," see Satan allegorically as representing God's self-doubt?[3] Or is God merely supremely self-confident and whimsical? But the tone of the story is the tone of folk-tale, where one simply does not ask such questions, one simply goes along with the entertaining-and-moral narrative.

The Poetry

Here, however, the poetry erupts. It erupts from agony, puncturing the surface of the text and pouring forth like lava, like the boils that have ruptured Job's skin, like an interior sickness. His abused body not merely speaks but wails, in an effort to make itself heard. The sufferer curses his birth. The whole of chapter 3 is a hyperbolic outpouring of his wish to die:

> Let the day perish in which I was born, and the night
> in which it was said, there is a man child conceived. Let

that day be darkness; let not God regard it from above, neither let the light shine upon it. Let darkness and the shadow of death stain it; let a cloud dwell upon it; let the blackness of the day terrify it. . . . Why died I not from the womb? Why did I not give up the ghost when I came out of the belly? Why did the knees prevent me? Or why the breasts that I should suck? For now I should have lain still and been quiet, I should have slept: then had I been at rest, with kings and counselors of the earth . . . or with princes . . . as infants which never saw light. There the wicked cease from troubling; and there the weary be at rest. . . . The small and the great are there. . . . Wherefore is light given to him that is in misery, and life unto the bitter in soul? . . . For my sighing cometh before I eat, and my roarings are poured out like the waters. (3.2–24)

His friends are shocked. Despair is an act of blasphemy. Yet Job sits naked upon his ash heap and despairs. And so the passionate poetic debate opens. At first his friends attempt to remind him, gently, that the innocent never perish, that God destroys only the wicked, that if a man accepts God's chastening he will be able to laugh at famine and war, have children "as the grass of the earth," and live to a ripe old age. "Shall mortal man be more just than God? Shall a man be more pure than his maker?" (4.17) asks Eliphaz the Temanite, thinking he is only saying what everyone knows. But Job will have none of their nostrums. "No doubt but ye are the people, and wisdom shall die with you," he retorts ironically. "But I have understanding as well as you; I am not inferior to you: yea, who knoweth not such things as these?" (12.2–3) The more his pious friends repeat the conventional wisdom, the more outraged he becomes. He roars his grief, he insists on his innocence, he recalls the time "when the Almighty was yet with me, when my children were about me" (29.5) and how he used to support the poor, the fatherless, the widow, how he was eyes to the blind and feet to the lame, how everyone respected him. He alternates between beseeching "have pity on me, have pity on me, O ye my friends" (19.21) and attacking them as accusers, "Miserable comforters are you all" (16.1), "Suffer me that I may speak, and after that I have spoken, mock on" (21.2)—while they attack him back, describing again and again the doom of the wicked: "he shall perish forever like his own dung. . . . He shall fly away as a dream . . . his meat in his bowels is turned. . . . He hath swallowed down riches, and he shall vomit them up again" (20.7–15), and so on. As readers, of course, we are constantly aware of the irony because we know more than any participant in this dialogue of the deaf can know.

As the argument heats, Job not only vindicates himself, he assails God: "It is all one; therefore I say he destroys both the blameless and the wicked. When disaster brings sudden death, he mocks at the calamity of the innocent. The earth is given into the hand of the wicked; he covers the eyes of its judges—if it is not he, who then is it?" (9.22–24). "Why do the wicked live on, reach old age, and grow mighty in power? Their children are established in their presence, and their offspring before their eyes. Their houses are safe from fear, and no rod of God is upon them" (21.7–29). The "wicked are spared in the day of calamity and are rescued in the day of wrath" (21.30). The friends insist that Job must have secretly sinned or he wouldn't be suffering and that no mortal has the right to question God. Job, scraping his scabs, denies any wrongdoing. Goaded by his body's experience of pain, his knowledge of the world's pain, the remorseless remoteness of this being who evidently exterminates both honest and wicked, and the piety of these sanctimonious friends, he calls God to account. "Though he slay me, yet will I trust in him; but I will maintain my own ways before him" (13.15). What this tells us is that Job never ceases to believe in God's existence and power, and in fact he never ceases to worship God, but at the same time he also believes in himself. He stands up for himself. He hungers for presence and not absence. He demands law and justice instead of accident and chaos. "Oh that I knew where I might find him! that I might come even to his seat! I would order my cause before him, and fill my mouth with arguments." To all this, the answer is silence. The silence of God.[4] It is impossible not to quote Martin Buber on the stalemate of the Book of Job:

> Instead of his God, for whom he looks in vain, his God, who had not only put sufferings upon him but had also "hedged him in" until "His way was hid" from his eyes (3.23), there now came and visited him on his ash heap *religion,* which uses every act of speech to take away from him the God of his soul. Instead of the "cruel" and living God, to whom he clings, religion offers him a reasonable and rational God, a deity whom he, Job, does not perceive either in his own existence or in the world, and who obviously is not to be found anywhere save only in the very domain of religion.[5]

The Whirlwind

Suddenly, without preparation, the Lord finally answers Job out of the whirlwind: "Who is this that darkeneth counsel by words without knowledge? Gird up thy loins now like a man: for I will demand of thee, and answer thou me" (38.2–3). His magnificent speech seems designed to smash Job and mankind into humility by an overwhelming display of creative might. The depths of the sea, the breadth of the earth, the treasures of the snow, the sweet influences of the Pleiades, the rain that causes the bud to spring forth in desolate and waste ground—who controls all this? Is it Job who guides Arcturus? Did Job clothe the neck of the warhorse with thunder and enable him to mock at fear? Does Job command the eagle to mount and make her nest on high, to seek and seize the prey so that her young ones can suck up blood? Is Job prepared to instruct El Shaddai?

> Where wast thou when I laid the foundations of the earth? Declare, if thou hast understanding. Who hath laid the measure thereof, if thou knowest? Or who hath stretched the line upon it? Whereupon are the foundations thereof fastened? Or who laid the corner stone thereof; when the morning stars sang together, and all the sons of God shouted for joy? Or who shut up the sea with doors, when it brake forth, as if it had issued out of the womb? When I made the cloud the garment thereof, and thick darkness a swaddling band for it. . . . And said, Hitherto shalt thou come, but no further: and here shall thy proud waves be stayed? (38.4–11)

Where the anguish of Job is volcanic, the mockery of God is cosmic: Were you there, he seems to ask not only Job but all mankind, when I made the world? Have you an arm like God? I am the Creator! I am the Ruler! I am not just! I have nothing to do with justice! That is the essence of the Lord's reply, and it is very splendid to read, the verbal equivalent of a thermonuclear explosion.

Stephen Mitchell in the introduction to his translation of the Book of Job notes the cosmic humor of the Voice from the whirlwind and compares it to Krishna's response to Arjuna in the Baghavad-Gita, "in which that prince experiences, down to the marrow of his bones, the glory and the terror of the universe, all creation and all destruction, embraced in the blissful play of the Supreme Lord."[6] Nothing else in literature, sacred or profane, remotely approaches the sublimity of the torrential speech that the anonymous Hebrew poet has imagined God uttering. Dante in *The Divine Comedy* wisely does not attempt to make God talk. Milton in *Paradise Lost* does put words in the Lord's mouth, with the disastrous result of making God sound like a prim schoolmaster. But reading the voice from the whirlwind, we can believe that this is exactly how the Creator of the Universe would sound if we could hear him. Job, along with us, is reminded that the cosmos is not chaotic but orderly, and that its order is infinitely and awesomely beyond his (and our) comprehension.

In this invocation of a vast heaven and earth capped by nature red in tooth and claw, man does not even merit a mention. Job ultimately does speak, saying he cannot answer: "Behold, I am vile [another translation is 'of small account'] . . . I will lay my hand upon my mouth. Once have I spoke; but I will not answer: yea, twice, but I will proceed no further" (40.4–5). But the Lord's temper is up, he repeats "Gird up thy loins . . ." and launches into a description of Behemoth and Leviathan, gigantic mythic creatures derived from Babylonian and Canaanite mythology.[7] Behemoth can drink up a river, Leviathan is an unconquerable "king over all the children of pride" (40.34).

At the close of God's second theophanic speech, Job speaks for the last time, agreeing that the Lord can do anything and that he himself has uttered what he did not understand. The famous words that follow, "I have heard of thee by the hearing of the ear; but now mine eye seeth thee," imply awe; do they also imply the pointlessness of everything both he and his friends have said about God before now? Do they imply that he is actually, visually, *seeing* something in the whirlwind, not merely hearing the words we are reading, despite the fact that even Moses was told that no man can see God and live? Or is the point that no teaching or doctrine can ever have the impact of personal experience? Isaiah 2.1, announcing "The word which Isaiah the son of Amoz *saw* concerning Judah and Jerusalem" [italics mine] seems to imply this, yet it is still ambiguous.

Job's final sentence is even more ambiguous. The traditional translation, "Therefore I abhor [or despise] myself and repent in dust and ashes," forms the basis for most interpretations of the poem, according to which Job is finally admitting a wrongdoing. The idea of repentance, however, gives us a rather Christian translation of an extremely obscure passage. The verb *'em'as* elsewhere means "to reject" or "loathe," but the Hebrew supplies no object for the verb. "I despise myself" is translators' guesswork. "I recant," the Jewish Publication Society version, lets us imagine Job saying "I'm sorry I said anything," as any browbeaten person may do. The phrase *nihamti 'al* can mean "I am sorry about" or "I am sorry for," or (according to Mitchell) "I am comforted," which would make Job's final meaning that he has seen God, recognizes his own insignificance and is content to be dust and ashes—that is, to die. Jack Miles argues that Job's final words are purely ironic, a mock-submission, but in any case there will be no further argument.[8] The theophany, and the poem, close there. The Lord has revealed his magnificent amorality, beyond good and evil. He is at once the most extraordinary egotist and the most extraordinary esthete, who has created the beauty and order of the universe for his own gratification, not for ours. Job has accepted this—or appeared to accept it.

The Two Endings and the Open Book

And then, startlingly, the Book of Job returns to the story-telling mode in which it opens.

> After the Lord had spoken these words unto Job, the Lord said to Eliphaz the Temanite, My wrath is kindled against you, and against your two friends; for you have not spoken of me the thing that is right, as my servant Job has. Therefore take unto you now seven bullocks and seven rams, and go to my servant Job and offer up for yourselves a burnt offering; and my servant Job will pray for you: for him I will accept: lest I deal with you after your folly, in that you have not spoken of me the thing that is right, like my servant Job. (42.7–8)

The Lord then proceeds to make Job twice as rich as he was before, and we are told that he has another seven sons and three daughters, that he gives the daughters an inheritance along with their brothers, and that he lives a hundred and forty more years. At first reading, one simply blinks at this. Job has not exactly cursed God, but he has certainly challenged his goodness, whereas the pious friends have said all the usually correct things. What do we make of the Lord's about-face? If all we had of the Book of Job were the folktale, with a sort of missing middle, then it would make sense. It is generally agreed by scholars that the prose frame is older than the poetry—that, in other words, a tale existed about a patient Job who was tested by God, passed the test, and was rewarded. End of story.

But the Book of Job as we have it clearly vindicates man and his challenge; it is almost a divine apology. It is as if God were saying: It's true that I'm unjust, and that's the way I like it, and of course the conventional religion of your friends, which claims that I am just and that your suffering is justified, is false as you are well aware; but, do you know, you have embarrassed me a little. There. I hereby rebuke your friends, give you power over them, and make you even more blessed than you were before. In this version Job was right in attacking the Lord's justice. His friends were wrong in defending it. Orthodoxy is wrong. Heterodoxy is right.

The two apparently contradictory conclusions of the Book of Job do not constitute a unique phenomenon in the Bible. As many modern scholars have observed, the Bible seems to be rather fond of self-contradiction. At its commencement there are two versions of creation: in one, male and female are created in God's image after the creation of the cosmos, the earth, plant life and animal life (Genesis 1.1–27); and in the other one, man is formed of the dust of the ground, followed by the vegetation, then animal life, and only then— from Adam's rib—woman (Genesis 2.4–22). Two versions exist of how many of each kind of creature entered Noah's Ark: a pair of everything in Genesis 6.19–20, 7.8–9, 15, but seven of each "clean" beast and each bird, and pairs only of "unclean" beasts (Genesis 7.2–3). There are also two startlingly inconsistent versions of David's advent. In 1 Samuel 16.13, when Samuel anoints David, David is Jesse's youngest son and is looking after the sheep; in the David and Goliath story (1 Samuel 17.12–58), David is still a youth, and the episode ends with Saul learning that he is Jesse's son. Yet between these two passages appears the passage in which David is described by courtiers as "a mighty valiant man, and a man of war," who comes to live at court and relieves Saul of his depression by performing on the harp (1 Samuel 16.14–23).[9]

It is not enough to point out, rationally, that these and other pieces of biblical stitchery are the result of multiple

sources and hundreds of years of editing. For the text of the
Bible as we have it is more than the sum of its parts, and
its inconsistencies are also apertures. A purely coherent and
consistent Bible would never have been able to command the
millennia of loyalty that the Bible has commanded. It would
lack mystery. It would be reduced to the flattest sort of theology. We need the layering, the tension, even the absurdity
of scripture. Just at the stretched seams of the stitching—
where light pierces the seams?—we may be able to experience
God's paradoxical essence as the One of whom all contraries
are equally true, or as the binding energy that holds together
what would otherwise fly apart. "I form the light, and create
darkness: I make peace, and create evil: I the Lord do all these
things" (Isaiah 45.7).

In Job, the contradictions are not smoothly spliced; they
are thrown in our face.[10] The gaps between the frame and the
poem, between the two halves of the frame, and between the
debate and the theophany, make Job a supremely open book
in its form and its meaning. We are given three images of
God: first, the one who gives Satan the assignment of tor-
menting Job; second, the Creator and Sustainer of the Universe; and finally, the God of the frame story epilogue who
rewards Job for telling the unpleasant truth about him. We
can never reconcile these parts; they cling together and pull
apart at the same time. Even more disturbingly, it seems that
all the versions of God have one thing in common: they represent him as Ego, as tyrant who cares primarily about his
mighty self and what human beings do or do not think of
him! What then does it signify that the poetry of the Book
of Job closes with God's challenger humbled, while the prose
frame closes with the challenger rewarded and the orthodox
punished? It seems to me here too that at least three possibilities are opened. One is that we should insist on seeing

the anti-authoritarian strain within Judaism as a permanent spiritual value. Second, we might recognize that the text is telling us that God can *change*. Third, and most radically, we may decide that we mortals, not God, are the source of morals, ethics, justice—that if justice is ever to be established on earth, it is we who are responsible for it.

Two Endings, Three Openings

From the wellspring of the Book of Job there flows a river of living waters of opposition to authority within Judaism that has affected all of Western history. The saying "two Jews, three opinions" marks Jewish culture as a culture that values argument. Is there another major religion in which human beings habitually argue with their God? Is there another major religion so preoccupied with dissent and with issues of social justice? The idea of interrogating God has streamed through Jewish literature for centuries. In the post-holocaust world it assumes major proportions. A rabbi in Elie Wiesel's *The Gates of the Forest* announces to his fellow concentration camp inmates, "I intend to convict God of murder, for he is destroying his people and the Law he gave them from Mount Sinai. I have irrefutable proof in my hands." In I. B. Singer's autobiographical *In My Father's Court,* the boy Isaac asks himself, "What did the Emperor of everything, the Creator of Heaven and Earth require? That he could go on watching soldiers fall on battlefields?" In Malamud's *The Fixer* occurs this dialogue: " 'Yakov,' said Shmuel passionately, 'Don't forget your God!' 'Who forgets who?' the fixer said angrily. 'What do I get from him but a bang on the head and a stream of piss in my face.' " Woody Allen captures an abiding pattern in Judaism when he remarks, "To you I'm an atheist. To God, I'm the loyal opposition." Sarah Ironson, the newly deceased Yiddishe-grandma of Tony Kushner's *Angels in America,* concurs: "You should struggle with the Almighty." *"Azoy toot a Yid,"* she adds: "It's the Jewish way." Like Job, the Jewish writers who challenge God typically do so in tones of acute intimacy—as if engaged in a sparring match with a powerful and crude yet somehow amenable uncle.

In attempting to understand this combination of intimacy and resistance, we may remember that historical Judaism originates in a slave rebellion and an advocacy of freedom that continue to resound in the aspirations and rhetoric of oppressed people throughout the world.[11] The role of the prophets includes a steady attack on the corruptions of Israelite ruling classes, sparing neither kings nor priests. Notwithstanding the centrality of ritual in the Israelite community, Isaiah, for example, is the mouthpiece of a God who two and a half millennia ago says, "I hate, I despise your offerings" and demands that his people feed the hungry, clothe the naked, and help the oppressed. Social justice as opposed to whatever authority resists it, including the authority of God himself, is a core motivation in Jewish history.

Following the destruction of the second Temple and throughout the history of the Diaspora, Jewish questioning has taken at least two different forms. As a marginal population Jewish writers have been social critics; and as a people whose survival depended on a Book and not a territory they developed intellectual institutions whereby a life of continual study and constant reinterpretation of that Book was the highest vocation to which a man (though not of course a woman) could aspire.

This brings me, if I may be permitted a digression, to the question of Job's wife. If Job represents human consciousness at a moment of crisis when orthodox piety is seen to be inadequate, what does his wife represent? In the legalistic terms which are so central to the book of Job, the wife does not even exist. As Harold Schweizer points out, "Job's wife has never owned any of the 'seven thousand sheep, and three thousand camels, and five hundred yoke of oxen, and five hundred she asses, and a very great household.'" Consequently "her suffering remains redundant,"[12] of no significance to the plot. She has no name of her own to begin with, and after her furious one-liner she never appears in the text again. But when I think of the supposedly happy ending, in which Job has ten nice new sons and daughters to replace the ones God killed off on a bet, I feel I am hearing a scream thousands of years old, or as if that scream inhabits my own throat. For I too am a mother. To me, the reparation offered in the epilogue is obscene. I imagine that one day Job's wife (that is to say, collective womankind) will gather the *chutzpah* to question God the way Abraham did, the way Jeremiah did, the way her husband did. I try to imagine her confrontation with God, and what she demands as reparation.[13] That day is not yet, and may not be for centuries. Yet the Book of Job asks me to imagine it. Perhaps the Book of Job asks me to imagine all those who have been silenced, all who have been consigned to nonentity, at last finding their voices, at last demanding response. The poor, the illiterate, the sexually deviant, the victims of war and violence, the animals, the earth itself . . .

Second, the Book of Job compels me to see God as a being who changes—and changes in response to us, dust and ashes though we are. Jung's *Answer to Job* develops this idea brilliantly to explain not only the advent, but also the failure, of Christianity. For Jung, the God of Job, and of the Old Testament as a whole, is "the totality of inner opposites—and this is the indispensable condition for his tremendous dynamism, his omniscience and omnipotence. . . . He is everything in its totality; therefore, among other things, he is total justice and also its total opposite." But Jung asserts that "a curious change . . . comes over Yahweh's behavior after the Job episode" in which it has become clear that "Job stands morally higher than Yahweh . . . the creature has surpassed the creator" so that the latter is forced into moral consciousness and ultimately must regenerate himself by becoming Man. "The encounter with the creature changes the creator." [14] Jung goes on to argue, however, that the attempt of Christianity to imagine a purely loving God fails, as is evidenced by the bloodthirsty apocalyptic visions at the close of the New Testament. From the perspective of the twenty-first century, with our knowledge of the history of the Crusades, the Inquisition, the centuries of devastating religious wars in Europe, not to mention the Holocaust, one can only agree. Writing in the 1950s, Jung was addressing, through the Job story, the dark side of both God and man in the wake of World War II. In a more recent version of the same idea, Jack Miles in *God: A Biography* depicts the God of Genesis through Kings II, and on through the prophets, as a being who is "not immutable," who changes and develops, who responds to experience, and whose response to his encounter with Job is uncanny:

> God's last words are those he speaks to Job, the human being who dares to challenge not his physical power but his moral authority. Within the Book of Job itself, God's climactic and overwhelming reply seems to silence Job. But reading from the end of the book of Job onward, we see that it is Job who has somehow silenced God. [15]

The books that follow Job in the order of the Hebrew Bible are Song of Songs, Ruth, Lamentations, Ecclesiastes, Esther, Daniel, Ezra, Nehemiah, and 1 and 2 Chronicles. Except for a

few occasions in Chronicles, which repeat material from earlier books, God is spoken of but ceases to speak, and indeed to
act. For Miles, the volatile and irritable Lord who has dominated human history goes into hiding. Is it a coincidence that
God's post-Job silence seems to duplicate on a large scale what
happens after Genesis 22, Abraham's near-sacrifice of Isaac,
on God's orders? Following this famous and disturbing episode, the Lord never again speaks to Abraham. Can Job's description of himself as "dust and ashes" be intended to remind
God, and the reader, that Abraham uses the same phrase of
himself in his bargaining-with-God episode (Genesis 18.27)?
Miles's subsequent book, *Christ: A Crisis in the Life of God,*
sees the Incarnation as a consequence of God's need to take
responsibility for evil: "The world is a great crime, and someone must be made to pay for it. Mythologically read, the New
Testament is the story of how someone, the right someone,
does pay for it." [16]

Jewish ideas of how God may change in response to Man
are different and varied. In Lurianic kabbala, *tikkun olam,* the
repair or mending of a broken world which is also a broken
Godhead, depends on human acts: the performance of commandments with *kavanah,* focused devotion, "raises the sparks"
of divine light that have been captured and hidden within the
material world, hastening the coming of the Messiah, the reunion of God with his Shekhinah, and the return of the entire universe to divinity. For contemporary activists *tikkun olam*
refers to acts of social responsibility, not the larger cosmologi-
cal realm of sacred acts—and on healing, not undoing, the
material world as we know it. Orthodox Jews and scholars of
Judaism alike dismiss this usage of the term as wildly untra-
ditional. Yet traditions change, traditions grow. Can we be so
certain that the realm of the spirit is distinct from the realm of
the body? I cling to the conviction aroused in me by the Song of

Songs, and experienced by lovers in all times and places, that the distinction is unreal. If a man and wife making love on the Sabbath model and even assist the union of God and his Shekhinah, it may well be that the performance of any good deed, any kindness, any act of compassion, accomplishes a portion of divine healing. In the book of Ruth, God's *chesed* and human generosity are somehow two sides of a single coin. Shakespeare's Lear comes to a comparable insight in the storm that shows him what a poor, bare, forked creature he is, and leads him to realize that he has taken "too little care" of the humble people of his realm: "Take physic, pomp," he cries to himself,

> Expose thyself to feel what wretches feel,
> That thou mayst shake the superflux to them,
> And show the heavens more just.

Is it only Lear's madness that makes him imagine that human ethics can "show" something about heavenly ethics?

As above, so below—and, yes, the reverse as well. The greatest aperture opened by the Book of Job is the doorway of moral choice, moral responsibility. According to Abraham Joshua Heschel, "God's dream is not to be alone, but to have humanity as a partner. . . . By whatever we do, by every act we carry out, we either advance or obstruct the drama of redemption." [17] The rabbis who created Talmud dwell on a passage in Deuteronomy that describes Torah, at the crucial moment when the Israelites were about to cross the river Jordan into the promised land:

> It is not too hard for you, neither is it far off. It is not in heaven, that you should say, "Who will go up to heaven, and bring it to us, that we may hear it and do it?" Neither is it beyond the sea, that you should say, "Who will

go over the sea for us, and bring it to us, that we may hear it and do it?" But the word is very near you; it is in your mouth and in your heart, so that you can do it. (Deuteronomy 30.11–14)

The equivalent utterance in Christian culture, "The kingdom of God is within you" (Luke 17.21), might well be an adaptation of this passage. What did the sages think this passage portended? They believed that it was up to *them* to decide what Torah meant, what the Law meant. There is a charming tale about a dispute between Rabbi Joshua and Rabbi Eleazar. Joshua, along with a majority of rabbis, took a more liberal view of a certain law, Eleazar a more strict view. Eleazar, appealing to God to vindicate him, said that if his interpretation was right, the walls of the study hall should fall in, a carob tree should uproot itself, and water should flow backward. All these miracles happened, but Joshua had the last word, by quoting "it is not in heaven," at which point a voice from above announced that Eleazar had lost. The majority ruled. It is said that God chuckled at this result, declaring, "My children have defeated me, my children have defeated me."

The rabbinical mind was quite able to suppose that human beings could teach God a thing or two about ethics. One of the most beautiful midrashim in Talmud tells that when Jerusalem was sacked by Babylon in 587 BCE and the people were going into exile, all the patriarchs went in turn before the Holy One in heaven to beg that he would relent and permit the Jews to return to their land. They all pleaded their merit, but God refused. Then the matriarch Rachel came before him. She reminded God that when she was betrothed to Jacob but her sister Leah was married to him by trickery she ultimately forgave her sister and they were reconciled. If she, Rachel, could overlook such a betrayal, could not God overlook the wrongdoings of Israel? God then agreed to let the people return from exile after fifty years; and it was so. Could there be a finer example of human-invented ethics producing a shift in the mind of God?

Something deeply ingrained in Jewish tradition seems to tell us, almost subliminally, that we cannot ultimately rely on God for moral guidance. We are in the world, and its problems are in our lap. Hillel is the sage who responded to the Roman who asked him to define Torah while standing on one foot. "Do not do to another," he is said to have replied, "what you do not want done to yourself. That is the whole of the law. The rest is commentary. Now go and study." He was also responsible for one of my favorite Jewish sayings: "If I am not for myself, who is for me? If I am for myself alone, what am I? and if not now, when?" The great Israeli poet Yehuda Amichai may have had a similar idea in his early poem, "God has Pity on Kindergarten Children." Notice how the poem begins with what sounds like pious faith, turns tragic almost immediately, but then turns again, from what God will do for us, to what we may possibly do for ourselves and one another:

> God has pity on kindergarten children.
> He has less pity on school children
> And on grownups he has no pity at all,
> he leaves them alone,
> and sometimes they must crawl on all fours
> in the burning sand
> to reach the first-aid station
> covered with blood.
>
> But perhaps he will watch over true lovers
> and have mercy on them and shelter them

like a tree over the old man
sleeping on a public bench.

Perhaps we too will give them
the last rare coins of charity
that Mother handed down to us
so that their happiness may protect us
now and on other days.[18]

At the very end of his life, in "When I die," Amichai imagines women washing his body, "And one of them will sing
God Full of Mercy . . . to remind God that mercy is born
of the womb."[19] Smilingly mocking the law by which men's
dead bodies must be washed by men, Amichai invites us to
ponder the fact that the term *rachmanes,* mercy or compassion,
a major attribute of the Holy One, is a cognate of the word
for womb.

"Justice, justice shalt thou pursue" (Deuteronomy 13.20).
Someone must choose justice. Someone must define it. If not
we, who? In the Book of Job, God is unable to choose justice
until Job challenges him—and even then we may remain skeptical. Is the restoration of one man's fortunes and the provision
of ten new children to replace ten murdered ones a sufficient
answer to the evil and suffering in the world? Does it take care
of human poverty, war, violence, and greed? It may be that
the Holy One waits for us to issue our challenge. Perhaps God
does not know how to be just until human beings demand it.
Then he knows. Then he responds. Or perhaps, after all, what
we name "God" is merely the laws of physics, the magnificent
laws of physics, and then the adorable laws of biology. And
finally, circuit by ticking circuit through the neural nets, the
exquisite laws of conscience. Conscience, gradually evolving.
Here is something that may finally command belief.

AFTERWORD

Revelation is never something over and done with or gone for good or in danger of slipping away into the past; it is ongoing.

—GERALD R. BRUNS, "MIDRASH AND ALLEGORY"

A t a crucial moment in his life, the patriarch Jacob wrestles with a mysterious stranger, commonly understood to be an angel. They wrestle all night, neither one winning. As dawn approaches, the stranger says, "Let me go, for dawn is coming." Jacob replies, "I will not let you go unless you bless me" (Genesis 32.26). The stranger then blesses Jacob with his new name, Israel, declaring that he has fought with God and with men, and has prevailed. Next to my front door hangs an etching of these two figures wrestling, which I made when I was twenty-two, in an art class. Jacob is struggling hard while the angel is smiling. The etching's title is Jacob's demand for blessing. I loved that sentence. It seemed to me that a game was being played, in which the angel was waiting for Jacob to say exactly those words. I did not anticipate that, decades later, much of my own life would be spent as a woman writer wrestling with the Bible, recognizing its masculine and authoritarian bias, and nonetheless attempting to wrestle a blessing from it.

These are, as I have said, one person's interpretations. They bear the weight of personal engagement, since the Bible is both a primary source of my most strongly held values and a source of much that I deplore and struggle against. It is a priceless hoard of literature, whose poetry and stories are endlessly compelling. Finally, it marks, for me, the point in Western culture where human life, human language, and the human experience of the divine, most fully converge. I can learn from it. I can wrestle with it. It fights back, and we both grow stronger. As a Jew, I believe that the Hebrew Bible, and God in the Bible, *want* to be wrestled with. This is how they stay alive. This is why the sages say, "There is always another interpretation."

I have been analytical; I have been personal. To take scripture personally and analytically is not to disrespect it. On the contrary. As the scholar Gerald Bruns argues, when we read the Bible, "if the text does not apply to us it is an empty text . . . . Although the text was composed in a situation very different from our own, it must be taken in relation to *our* situation if it is to have any force." [1] Readers who use the Bible both as a window into reality and as a mirror into the self will emerge with a sharper understanding of themselves, their worlds, their spiritual paths, their multiple choices.

If the unexamined life is not worth living, attention to Biblical writings makes an excellent conduit to self-examination. When I read the Song of Songs, the sixteen-year-old in me revives. Once again I am in love for the first time, body and soul are fused, and the world itself is holy. When I read Ruth, I suspend disbelief, relax and enjoy a tale in which humanity trumps nationality. Reading Psalms is again completely different; these white-hot poems go straight to the limbic system. Love, terror, hate, joy, trust, doubt, rage, need—my emotions are laid out like blueprints on a draughtsman's table. Some of them are exalted. Others are horribly destructive. Then when I read Ecclesiastes I am intellectually exhilarated

and feel capable of achieving serenity, when I read Jonah I
come face to face with my depressive and suicidal impulses,
and when I read Job I am the descendant of East European
Jews who thought it was up to them to make the world a
better place. Reading Job I am the person who attends dem-
onstrations, signs petitions, and believes in *tikkun olam,* the
mending of the world. I am also the wife and mother who is
silenced in Job, and must ultimately speak.

I am these selves; my readers, I assume, are equally complex and contradictory. Meanwhile, we live in a world in crisis. Perhaps immersing ourselves in some of the wisest writing ever written will help us know ourselves and the world
better. Let us not try to simplify reality. Let us not use our
sacred texts as a security blanket or a blindfold, much less a
weapon. We need not let the Bible be the property of people
who cannot imagine a connection between spirituality and
sex, or skepticism and joy, or Us and Them. Love is as strong
as death, says the Song of Songs. We might try taking that
seriously. The angry tide of fundamentalisms flooding the
world can perhaps be overcome, not by denying the channel
of the spirit altogether, but by widening it. We (and by "we" I
mean both secular and religious, both men and women) need
to claim the life of the spirit along with the lives of body and
mind. For the love of God, I would like to see in my lifetime, or the lifetimes of my granddaughters, a world in which
thought is free and in which there are new sacred songs, along
with a new idea of what is sacred. If they choose to be believers in a God, I hope my granddaughters find themselves a
God worth worshiping, with an ethics worth pursuing. I hope
that they and their generation, or some generation soon after
them, will come to wrestle God and man, like Jacob, and pre-
vail. That would be something new under the sun.

Some Further Reading

Alta, *The Shameless Hussy: Selected Stories, Essays and Poems.* Trumansburg, N.Y.: Crossing Press, 1980.

Alter, Robert, ed. *The Five Books of Moses: A Translation with Commentary.* New York: W.W. Norton, 2004.

Alter, Robert, and Frank Kermode, eds. *The Literary Guide to the Bible.* Cambridge, Mass.: Harvard University Press, 1987.

Amichai, Yehuda. *Open Closed Open.* Translated by Chana Bloch and Chana Kronfeld. New York: Harcourt, 2000.

————. *The Selected Poetry.* Translated by Chana Bloch and Stephen Mitchell. New York: Harper & Row, 1986.

Bachmann, Christina, and Celina Spiegel, eds. *Out of the Garden: Women Writers on the Bible.* New York: Ballantine, 1994.

Barton, George Aaron. *Ecclesiastes: A Critical and Exegetical Commentary.* Edinburgh: T & T Clark, 1908.

Bloch, Ariel, and Chana Bloch. *The Song of Songs: A New Translation.* New York: Random House, 1995; reprinted, Modern Library Classics, 2006.

Bonhoefer, Dietrich. "Vengeance and Deliverance." In *A Testament to Freedom: the Essential Writings of Dietrich Bonhoeffer,* edited by Geffrey B. Kelly and F. Burton Nelson. New York: HarperCollins, 1990.

Book of Job. Translated and with an introduction by Stephen Mitchell. New York: HarperCollins, 1992.

Boyarin, Daniel. *Carnal Israel: Reading Sex in Talmudic Culture.* The New Historicism: Studies in Cultural Politics 25. Berkeley: University of California Press, 1993.

Brenner, Athalya. *The Song of Songs.* Sheffield, Eng.: Sheffield Academic Press, 1989.

Buber, Martin. *The Prophetic Faith.* New York: Macmillan, 1949.

Carr, Jon. *The Erotic Word: Sexuality, Spirituality, and the Bible.* New York: Oxford University Press, 2003.

Campbell, E. F., Jr. *Ruth.* Anchor Bible. Garden City, N.Y.: Doubleday, 1975.

Celan, Paul. *Selected Poems and Prose.* Translated by John Felstiner. New York: Norton, 2001.

Cohen, A. D. "The Tragedy of Jonah." *Judaism* 21 (1972): 164–175.

Cooper, David. *God is a Verb: Kabbalah and the Practice of Mystical Judaism.* New York: Riverhead Books, 1997.

Dickinson, Emily. *Complete Poems.* Edited by Thomas H. Johnson. Boston: Little, Brown, 1980.

Eilberg-Schwartz, Howard. *God's Phallus: and Other Problems for Men and Monotheism.* Boston: Beacon Press, 1994.

Exum, J. Cheryl. *Plotted, Shot and Painted: Cultural Representations of Biblical Women.* Sheffield, England: Sheffield Academic Press, 1996.

———. *The Song of Songs: A Commentary.* Louisville, Ky.: Westminster; John Knox Press, 2005.

Fewell, Danna, and David Gunn. *Compromising Redemption: Relating Characters in the Book of Ruth.* Louisville, Ky.: Westminster Press, 1990.

Fox, Michael V. *A Time to Tear Down, A Time To Build Up: A Rereading of Ecclesiastes.* Grand Rapids, Mich.: William B. Eerdmans Publishing Co., 1999.

Freud, Sigmund. "Humour." *Abstracts of the Standard Edition of the Complete Psychological Works,* edited by Carrie Lee Rothget. New York: International Universities Press, 1973.

Ginzburg, Louis. *The Legends of the Jews.* Philadelphia: Jewish Publication Society, 1913.

Good, Edwin M. *In Turns of Tempest: A Reading of Job.* Stanford, Calif.: Stanford University Press, 1990.

Greenfield, Jonas C. "The Holy Bible and Canaanite Literature." In *The Literary Guide to the Bible,* edited by Robert Alter and Frank Kermode. Cambridge, Mass.: Harvard University Press, 1987.

Heschel, Susanna, ed. *On Being a Jewish Feminist,* New York: Schocken Books, 1983.

Hopkins, Gerard Manley. *Poems.* London and New York: Oxford University Press, 1967.

Hubbard, R. *The Book of Ruth.* Grand Rapids, Mich.: William B. Eerdmans, 1988.

Kates, J. A., and G. Twersky Reimer, eds. *Reading Ruth: Contemporary Women Reclaim a Sacred Story.* New York: Ballantine Books, 1994.

Kristeva, Julia. *Tales of Love.* Translated by Leon S. Roudiez. New York: Columbia University Press, 1987.

Jung, Carl. *Answer to Job.* Translated by R.F.C. Hull. Princeton, N.J.: Princeton University Press, 1973.

————. *Symbols of Transformation.* New York: Pantheon, 1956.

Lacocque, André, and Pierre-Emmanuel Lacocque. *Jonah: A Psycho-Religious Approach to the Prophet.* Columbia: University of South Carolina Press, 1990.

Layton, Anson. *Arguing with God: a Jewish Tradition.* Northvale, N.J., and London: J. Aronson, 1990.

Lerner, Michael. *Jewish Renewal: A Path to Healing and Transformation.* New York: G. P. Putnam's Sons, 1994.

Limburg, James. *Jonah: A Commentary.* London: SCM Press, 1993.

Longman, Tremper, III. *Fictional Akkadian Autobiography: A Generic and Comparative Study.* Winona Lake, Indiana: Eisenbrans, 1991.

Madsen, Catherine. "Notes on God's Violence." *CrossCurrents* 51.2 (Summer 2001): 229–256.

Magonet, Jonathan. "Whither Shall I Go From Your Spirit: A Study of the Book of Jonah." London: The Guild of Pastoral Psychology. Guild Lecture No. 208, Colmore Press, n.d.

Maslow, Abraham. *Toward a Psychology of Being.* New York: D. Van Nostrand, 1968.

McFague, Sallie. *Models of God: Theology for an Ecological, Nuclear Age.* Fortress Press, 1987.

Merkin, Daphne. "The Women in the Balcony: on Rereading the Song of Songs." In *Out of the Garden: Women Writers on the Bible,* edited by Christina Büchmann and Celina Spiegel. New York Random House, 1994.

Miles, Jack. *Christ: A Crisis in the Life of God.* New York: Random House, 2001.

————. *God: A Biography.* New York: Random House, 1996.

Murphy, Roland. *The Song of Songs; a Commentary.* Minneapolis: Fortress Press, 1990.

Norris, Kathleen. "The Paradox of the Psalms." In *Out of the Garden: Women Writers on the Bible.* Edited by Christina Bachmann and Celina Spiegel. New York: Ballantine, 1994.

Ostriker, Alicia. *Feminist Revision and the Bible.* Cambridge, Mass.: Blackwell Publishers, 1992.

————. *The Nakedness of the Fathers.* Boston: Beacon Press, 1994.

————. *The Volcano Sequence.* Pittsburgh: University of Pittsburgh Press, 2002.

Ozick, Cynthia. "Notes Toward Finding the Right Question." *On Being a Jewish Feminist,* edited by Susannah Heschel. New York: Schocken Books, 1983.

Pagels, Elaine. *The Origin of Satan.* New York: Random House, 1995.

Pardes, Ilana. *Counter-Traditions in the Bible: A Feminist Approach.* Cambridge: Harvard University Press, 1992.

Patai, Raphael. *The Hebrew Goddess.* New York: Avon, 1978.

Perry, T. A. *Dialogues with Kohelet: The Book of Ecclesiastes, Translation and Commentary.* University Park: Pennsylvania State University Press, 1993.

Plaskow, Judith. "Spirituality and Politics: Lessons from B'not Esh." *Tikkun.* 10. 3 (May–June 1995).

———. *Standing Again at Sinai: Judaism From a Feminist Perspective.* San Francisco: Harper & Row, 1990.

Pope, Marvin H., ed. *The Songs of Songs.* Garden City, N.Y.: Doubleday, 1977.

Robertson, David. "The Book of Job: A Literary Study." *Soundings* 56 (1973): 446–469.

Rosen, Norma. *Accidents of Influence: Writing as a Woman and a Jew in America.* Albany: State University of New York Press, 1992.

Rumi, Jelalludin. *Open Secret: Versions of Rumi.* Translated by John Moyne and Coleman Barks. Putney, Vt.: Threshold Books, 1984.

Sasson, Jack M. *The Anchor Bible: Jonah, A New Translation with Introduction, Commentary, and Interpretation.* New York: Doubleday, 1990.

Schulman, Grace. "The Song of Songs: Love is Strong as Death." In *Congregation: Contemporary Writers Read the Jewish Bible,* edited by David Rosenberg. New York: Harcourt Brace Javonovich, 1987.

Schweizer, Harold. *Suffering and the Remedy of Art.* Albany: State University of New York Press, 1997.

Shapiro, Rami. *The Way of Solomon: A New Interpretation.* San Francisco: HarperCollins, 2000.

Sherwood, Yvonne. *A Biblical Text and Its Afterlives: the Survival of Jonah in Western Culture.* Cambridge: Cambridge University Press, 2000.

Stanton, Elizabeth Cady. *The Woman's Bible.* 2 vols. New York: European Publishing Co. 1892, 1895.

———. *The Woman's Bible Commentary: Expanded Edition.* Edited by Carol Newsom and Sharon H. Ringe. Louisville: Westminster John Knox Press, 1998.

Stevens, Wallace. *The Collected Poems.* New York: Knopf, 1954.

Sutherland, Robert. *Putting God on Trial: the Biblical Book of Job.* Victoria, Canada: Trafford, 2004. Available online.

Trible, Phyllis. *God and the Rhetoric of Sexuality.* Philadelphia: Fortress Press, 1978.

Walzer, Michael. *Exodus and Revolution.* New York: Basic Books, 1985.

Whybray, R. N. *The New Century Bible Commentary: Ecclesiastes.* Grand Rapids, Mich.: William B. Eerdmans, 1989.

Zornberg, Aviva. "The Concealed Alternative." In *Reading Ruth: Contemporary Women Reclaim a Sacred Story,* edited by J. A. Kates and G. Twersky Reimer. New York: Ballantine Books, 1994.

Notes

Preface

1. For example, virtually no modern translation correctly renders the opening line of the Song of Songs as does the KJV: "Let him kiss me with the kisses of his mouth; for thy love is better than wine." See my discussion of this subject in my chapter on the Song of Songs. On the other hand, the KJV's "Vanity, vanity, all is vanity" at the opening of Ecclesiastes, is brilliant, and has been incalculably influential in English literature and, dare one say, culture. However, it is deeply misleading as a translation. Robert Alter's discussion of the comparative defects of the KJV and modern translations, in the introduction to his translation of *The Five Books of Moses,* is the best exposition I know of the subject.

Introduction

1. Robert Alter and Frank Kermode, eds., *The Literary Guide to the Bible,* 12.

2. Sallie McFague, *Models of God,* 19. McFague proposes that we think of the world as God's body rather than God's kingdom and constructs possible models of God as mother, lover, and friend, rather than mighty father and king.

3. I take the term from Ilana Pardes's *Counter-Traditions in the Bible* and with the understanding that the Bible includes not only counter-texts of vastly different scope, ranging from a phrase or a brief episode to an entire book, but that there are many and varied *sorts* of counter-texts. Pardes's examples of brief passages are Genesis 4:1, in which Eve says she has gotten a son with God, and Exodus 4:24–26, in which Moses' wife Zipporah saves his life when God tries to kill him. Pardes also gives full-scale interpretations of the Song of Songs and the Book of Ruth.

The Song of Songs: A Holy of Holies

1. The canonization process remains shrouded in the mists of antiquity for all the books of the Jewish Bible, not only for the Song. Robert Alter, in the introduction to his and Frank Kermode's *Literary Guide to*

the Bible, 12–13, speculates, with the Song, Job, and Ecclesiastes in mind, that "the selection was at least sometimes impelled by a desire to preserve the best of ancient Hebrew literature rather than to gather the consistent normative statements of a monotheistic party line." Athalya Brenner, *The Song of Songs,* 13–14, lists as the probable reasons for its canonization the attribution to Solomon; its popularity among the people; and, most important, the endorsement of its allegorical interpretation as the "officially valid exegesis." Ilana Pardes, *Countertraditions in the Bible: A Feminist Approach,* 124–127, suggests further that the Song "had the potential of filling a religious need" for a sense of the otherwise incorporeal God's more intimate presence, and as a counterweight to "the misogynist prophetic degradation of the nation [and of women]." See also Marvin H. Pope, ed., *The Songs of Songs,* 18–19, Roland Murphy, *The Song of Songs: A Commentary,* 5–6, and especially J. Cheryl Exum, *The Song of Songs: A Commentary,* 70–73. Exum points out (p. 77) that the Song lends itself to allegorical interpretation precisely because it is so effective as love poetry that can "represent any and all lovers" and invites all readers to "identify their experience with that of the protagonists." Exum's volume also includes an excellent fresh translation and commentary.

2. Pope, *The Song of Songs,* 19.

3. Ariel Bloch and Chana Bloch, *The Song of Songs: A New Translation,* 30.

4. Ibid., 11.

5. Daniel Boyarin, *Carnal Israel: Reading Sex in Talmudic Culture.*

6. Pope, *Song of Songs,* 165.

7. Raphael Patai, *The Hebrew Goddess,* 267; 325n 60.

8. Boyarin, *Carnal Israel,* 122–123.

9. Brenner, *Song of Songs,* 33; see also 65, 89–90.

10. See Pope, *Song of Songs,* 54–89, 145–153.

11. Judith Plaskow, *Standing Again at Sinai: Judaism From a Feminist Perspective,* 51, 194. Plaskow's chapter 5, "Toward A New Theology of Sexuality," notes that, on the one hand, rabbinic support of sex within marriage includes the obligation of men to satisfy their wives sexually; on the other hand, women are unclean and sexually dangerous temptresses. A parallel ambivalence pertains to sexual symbolism and the sacred. On the one hand, the Song of Songs, the mystic symbolism of the Shekhinah as God's bride, and the belief that intercourse between man and wife hastens their divine reunion; on the other, an asexual God, woman as possession rather than equal partner, and the insistence on separation rather than mingling of the sexes, in matters both sacred and domestic. Among the

writers and thinkers Plaskow cites as working to reclaim the connection between sexuality and the sacred, and to reimagine female sexuality as positive, are Adrienne Rich, Beverly Harrison, Audre Lorde, Rachel Adler, T. Drorah Setel, Lynn Gottleib, James Nelson, Phyllis Trible, and Arthur Green. They include Jews and non-Jews, men and women.

12. Roland Murphy, *The Song of Songs: A Commentary*, 39.

13. Ibid., 104–105.

14. Grace Schulman, "The Song of Songs: Love is Strong as Death," 358–359. See also Stephen Mitchell's brief but seductive foreword in the 2006 Modern Library reprint of the Bloch and Bloch translation.

15. Jon Carr, *The Erotic Word: Sexuality, Spirituality, and the Bible*.

16. Contrast Julia Kristeva, who claims in "A Holy Madness: He and She" in *Tales of Love*, 113, that the lovers are actually in love with each other's *absence*, that "the presence of the loved one is fleeting . . . no more than an expectation . . . an unceasing rush," and that sexual satisfaction does not in fact take place between them. Daphne Merkin calls the Song "this infamously titillating text" and also claims that "the two amorphously defined lovers . . . never come close to consummating their relationship" (247, 250). One may speculate that Kristeva and Merkin do not know Hebrew. Among the passages which represent lovemaking as either taking place at present or being happily remembered, are 2:3–6, 2:16; 5:1, 6:2–3; 6:11–12. See also the Blochs's straightforward demonstration that "the sexual relationship between the two lovers is not just yearned for—as has often been assumed—but actually consummated" (pp. 3–4, 178).

17. See Exum, *Song of Songs*, 128–129.

18. See ibid., 255–259 on this difficult passage.

19. Bloch and Bloch, *Song of Songs*, 125.

20. Merkin seems disconcerted by the "remarkably diffuse boundaries," the "emotional lability," and the absence of gender-stereotyped behavior in the poem (239–242). Plaskow, *Standing at Sinai* (119), makes the point that "since different forms of hierarchy and oppression intersect with and reinforce one another, none finally will be abolished until all have fallen."

21. Judith Plaskow, "Spirituality and Politics: Lessons from B'not Esh," 32.

22. We are accustomed to the generalization that the woman in the Song of Songs stands for Israel; however, "Israel" signifies a *male* community perceiving itself as God's lover. Howard Eilberg-Schwartz, in his provocative and brilliant study *God's Phallus: and Other Problems for Men and Monotheism*, chapter 4, discusses the marriage metaphor in

Hosea, Jeremiah, and Ezekiel; he points out that "the images of a female Israel . . . were addressed primarily to men and conceptualized their male relationship to God. Men were encouraged to imagine themselves as married to and hence in a loving relationship with God." What did this imply for their masculinity? Chapter 7 discusses in detail rabbinical readings of the Song of Songs which feminize the figures of the patriarchs, Moses and Aaron, David, and indeed all observant Jewish males in relation to God as lover. Women, according to Eilberg-Schwartz, pose a threat not merely to male authority insofar as it emulates God's authority, but also to the male-male love relationship between men and God: if men "do not take their proper role as God's wives, then the human women are always ready to assume that role" (160). If men are metaphoric women in relation to God, then actual women must be excluded altogether from the circle of immediate spiritual relationship.

23. In her provocative essay "Notes Toward Finding the Right Question," originally published in *Lilith* in 1979, Cynthia Ozick claims that the exclusion of Jewish women from the ongoing creative and intellectual life of the Jewish people has been "a loss numerically greater than a hundred pogroms. . . . A loss culturally and intellectually more debilitating than a century of autos-da-fé; than a thousand evil bonfires of holy books." One might add that Jewish spirituality, as well, has denied itself half its potential.

The Book of Ruth and the Love of the Land

1. A first sharp foray is the feminist Elizabeth Cady Stanton's two-volume *The Women's Bible,* the work of Elizabeth Cady Stanton and a few friends, originally published in 1892 and 1895.

2. The view that Ruth was intended as polemic against the policy of Ezra and Nehemiah prohibiting interracial marriages, or against the theocratic party in post-exilic Jerusalem, is no longer popular. Several commentators see Ruth as a *non*polemical variant on what is usually taken to be a nationalist norm.

3. I use the New Jewish Publication Society translation of Ruth in this chapter, except where noted, as its modernity seems appropriate to the briskness of the storytelling.

4. E. F. Campbell, Jr., *Ruth,* 22–23, speculates that a professional "wise woman" storyteller might have authored the tale.

5. There is a figure and ground issue here, but the real question is deeper. Students tend to argue over whether the women's story in Ruth, with its emphasis on relationships, is or is not "co-opted" or "exploited" or "submerged" by the patriarchal narrative with its emphasis on genealogy.

The assumption is that female and male aspects of a culture are necessarily opposed, that their relationship can only be one of oppression. My own view is that the book's enduring attractiveness depends on an alternative dynamic which integrates its men and women characters, male and female principles, vertical and horizontal dimensions, so artfully that we cannot rightly claim dominance for one over the other. A parallel is Cheryl Exum's examination of how readers of the Book of Ruth commonly locate the weight of the tale *either* with the (implicitly lesbian) Ruth-Naomi relation *or* with the (heterosexual) Boaz and Ruth relation, and deny the importance of the other (*Plotted, Shot and Painted: Cultural Representations of Biblical Women*). My view is that the tale's cultural and spiritual excellence lies in the fact that it allows for polarized readings, but forcefully invites and supports integrated ones.

6. My students tend to see Ruth's declaration to Naomi as sincere and passionate, possibly sexual. Some are disturbed at Naomi's unresponsiveness; others are confident that she loves or comes to love Ruth. Either way, they identify emotionally with Ruth. They divide over their interpretations of Ruth-Boaz: some see Ruth as humiliatingly submissive, while others see her as successfully landing a fish. A few find the story touching, but nobody finds it romantic. Mature students tend to concentrate on Naomi. It has been suggested to me that Naomi would like to have caught Boaz for herself, but knew she was out of the running. All of which is to say: my students see the Book of Ruth as a complex, subtle, not simple, portrayal of relationships.

7. Phyllis Trible, *God and the Rhetoric of Sexuality*, 173.

8. An alternative and more cynical reading of the Naomi-Ruth relationship is advanced by Fewell and Gunn, *Compromising Redemption: Relating Characters in the Book of Ruth*. They posit a "less than altruistic Naomi" (83) who suspects that her daughters-in-law are responsible for the death of her sons, who fails to acknowledge Ruth's existence when she returns to Bethlehem, and who never becomes openly demonstrative toward her even when the townswomen chidingly remind her of Ruth's value.

9. Aviva Zornberg, "The Concealed Alternative," in J. A. Kates and G. Twersky Reimer, eds., *Reading Ruth: Contemporary Women Reclaim a Sacred Story*, 78.

10. R. Hubbard, *The Book of Ruth*, 72.

11. I thank my husband, J. P. Ostriker, for pointing out that other biblical women besides Ruth are enterprising, initiative-taking, and successful in their endeavors. Examples include Rebecca, the Tamar of Genesis, Abigail, and Esther.

Psalm and Anti-Psalm: A Personal Interlude

1. National Public Radio News Special, 3:00 PM ET, Sept. 11, 2001.
2. BBC World News, Sunday, Oct. 7, 2001, 22:31 GMT.
3. *The International Herald Tribune,* Saturday-Sunday, September 29–30, 2001, pp. 1, 4.
4. Jonas C. Greenfield, "The Holy Bible and Canaanite Literature," p. 552, quotes as one example of the kind of poetry from which our psalms sprang:

Now, your enemy, O Ba'al
 now, you smite your enemy
  you strike your adversary;
you will take your eternal kingdom
 your everlasting dominion.

5. Dietrich Bonhoefer, "Vengeance and Deliverance," *A Testament to Freedom: the Essential Writings of Dietrich Bonhoeffer,* 293–298.
6. Kathleen Norris, "The Paradox of the Psalms," *Out of the Garden: Women Writers on the Bible,* 221–233.
7. Catherine Madsen, "Notes on God's Violence," *Cross Currents* 51.2, 229–256.
8. *The Book of Job,* translated and with an introduction by Stephen Mitchell, xxi.
9. Mitchell, *Job,* xiv.
10. If so, this would be a very New Age Buddhism. As my Buddhist friend Michael Venditozzi points out to me, "I know no Buddhist (and no sane interpretation of Buddhism) that would leave out the dashing of the child's head. Quite the opposite, actually."
11. The work in progress described here was published as *The Volcano Sequence* (University of Pittsburgh Press, 2002).

Ecclesiastes as Witness

1. Luther was the first to argue that Solomon was not the author. Grotius regarded Ecclesiastes as an anthology of opinions of different sages. In the eighteenth century this view became common among scholars. Today almost everyone agrees that the title and epilogue(s) (12.9–14) are editorial additions, but otherwise no consensus exists. George Aaron Barton, *Ecclesiastes: A Critical and Exegetical Commentary,* surveys the possible editorial interpolations: the title given by an editor; the "says Ecclesiastes" of 1.2, 7.27 and 12.8; the interpolations of 12.9–13 which

speak of Ecclesiastes in the third person; passsages declaring God's rewards and punishments—2.26, 3.17, 7.18b, 26b, 29, 8.2b, 3a, 5, 6a, 11–13, 11.9b, 12.1a, 13—which all interrupt or contradict the chief ideas, or both, and which he suggests are the work of an orthodox glosser, a pharisee; also the parables in 4.5, 5.3, 5.7a, 7.1a, 3.5, 3.6–9, 11, 12, 19; 8.1, 9.17–18, 10.1–3, 10.8–14a, 15, 18, 19. My approach parallels that of Michael V. Fox, *A Time to Tear Down, A Time To Build Up: A Rereading of Ecclesiastes,* which argues that the contradictions in Ecclesiastes are essential to his meaning, but my conclusions differ.

2. T. A. Perry, *Dialogues with Kohelet: The Book of Ecclesiastes, Translation and Commentary,* 78, noting that Qoheleth takes masculine verbs except in 7.27, *amrah quoheleth,* suggests that if Harold Bloom can posit a female J, there is as good a reason to speak of a lady Qoheleth. I think this is intended ironically.

3. Rami Shapiro, *The Way of Solomon: A New Interpretation,* 1–2.

4. The KJV gives "vexation of spirit."

5. Q is investigating the condition of generic "man," *adam,* which can imply (as in Genesis 1.26–27), male and female, as against *ish,* which is necessarily male; a woman reader can take some slight comfort in this.

6. Tremper Longman, III, *Fictional Akkadian Autobiography: A Generic and Comparative Study,* 217, 219.

7. *Lev,* heart, is in biblical Hebrew the seat of the intellect as well as the affections; it often means "mind."

8. R. N. Whybray, *The New Century Bible Commentary: Ecclesiastes,* discussing the influence of Hellenism's cult of the individual on educated Jews, notes that Q cares only about the self, uniquely (in scripture) rejecting such central ideas as the value of progeny, and has no engagement with the good of the community or nation.

9. *Simchah,* which occurs eight times in Ecclesiastes, is variously translated pleasure, joy, mirth, enjoyment; *samach* and *sameach* are variously rendered enjoy oneself, find enjoyment, rejoice.

10. Whybray, *New Century Bible Commentary,* 66–73, argues that Q is quoting a familiar passage in order to make his own comments on it; he thinks Q's point is that God designates the correct times for things but that man cannot know what they are. Diana Lipton (personal correspondence) observes that there is a subtext of sexuality: *Hefetz,* usually translated "purpose" or "goal," can mean "desire." "A time to be born" may also mean "a time to give birth." Planting can imply insemination, *l'akor* may mean both "pluck up" and "be barren." The term for slaying, *harog,* implies a knife or sword; the word for healing could be a pun on a word for "withdraw." Stones, gathered or thrown, may be euphemistic

for genitals (cf. "getting your rocks off"). Finally, in "a time to speak," "speaking" in Talmud is also a euphemism for sex.

11. The meditative practice in Jewish mysticism which is designed to achieve the state of mind of selflessness, egolessness or *ayin*, nothing, in which one is emptied of ego and becomes a vehicle for divine will, is called *bittul ha-yesh*. See David A. Cooper, *God Is a Verb: Kabbalah and the Practice of Mystical Judaism*, 67, 214–215, 222–224. Note: I do not think of Qoheleth as a mystic. I think of him as halfway there, between a rock and a hard place.

12. Most of Qoheleth's nostrums and proverbs are rather bland. A nasty bit, however, is the mini-rant against the female sex in 7.26–28, which claims his soul has not found "one woman in a thousand," which I find intensely irritating and which is later contradicted in the advice to "live joyfully with the woman whom you love all the days of your life of mist which he has given you under the sun . . . for that is your portion in life" (8.9).

13. Whybray, *New Century Bible Commentary*, 166.

14. The sequence uncannily parallels a journey through Kabbala's four worlds or spheres of consciousness: *asiyah*, the world of physicality, which for Qoheleth would be bitter; *yetzirah*, the world of emotion which in Qoheleth is essentially a house of mourning; *beriyah*, the world of intellect which looking at itself is able to laugh; and finally *atzilut*, the world of spirit.

15. I feel it is legitimate to call Qoheleth post-modern; his claim that "there is nothing new under the sun" implies a view of history as eternal recurrence. If history is not linear but simply repeats itself, post-modernism has existed before and will again. So too with modernism, and Qoheleth has been labelled "modern" often enough. My point would be that wherever in history we happen to be, Qoheleth is there with us, hovering at the periphery of vision.

16. Perry, *Dialogues*, argues throughout that the book is structured as a debate which gives skepticism its due but upholds scriptural traditions.

17. Whybray's claim (*New Century Bible Commentary*, 76) that "it is not his purpose to attack the way in which God governs—or misgoverns—the world, but to ask what is the best response man can make in this situation," suggests that Whybray has come perilously close to recognizing how perilously close Ecclesiastes is to Job. Fox (*Time to Tear Down*, 49) asserts that Q "does not resign himself to injustice but is continually shocked by it [because] injustices are offensive to reason," and goes on to claim that "when belief in a grand causal order collapses, human reason and self-confidence fail with it. This failure is what God intends, for after

it comes fear, and fear is what God desires. . . . God allows us to build small meanings from the shards of reason." To me, however, it seems that *experience,* not "reason," is Q's core value, and that Q never claims to know what God intends.

18. Cf. Job's irony (12.2–3) answering the friends who have belabored him with familiar nostrums, "No doubt you are the people and wisdom shall die with you. But I have understanding as well as you; I am not inferior to you; who does not know such things as these?"

Jonah: The Book of the Question

1. See Yvonne Sherwood, *A Biblical Text and Its Afterlives: the Survival of Jonah in Western Culture,* for an exhaustive and entertaining study of "mainstream" and minority interpretations of Jonah down to the present day; see especially p. 105.

2. See James Limburg, *Jonah: A Commentary,* 105–106. Limburg's Appendices excerpt several texts from early Jewish and Christian commentaries on Jonah.

3. See Sherwood, *Biblical Text,* 104–105; Limburg, *Jonah,* 44.

4. Carl Jung, *Symbols of Transformation,* 205.

5. Sherwood, *Biblical Text,* 130–140, 166–167.

6. *Midrash Jonah* explains that this was accomplished by locking newborn calves away from their mothers, so that both calves and cows cried for each other.

7. Even as early as the Exodus, God's willingness to change his mind is made clear. When, after the episode of the Golden Calf, God is so infuriated that he declares he is going to "consume" all the Israelites with his "burning wrath" and start a new nation with Moses, Moses calms him down by reminding him of his promises to Abraham, Isaac, and Jacob, pointing out that if he destroys Israel, the Egyptians will think he delivered them from Egypt just to kill them; in other words, his reputation will suffer. On this occasion "God relented from the evil which he said he would do to his people" (Exodus 32.11–14).

8. In Sanhedrin 59a, BQ 38a, Aboda 3a, Sifra Shemoth 13, "When a non-Jew turns to God and repents, he becomes greater than the high priest, the day becomes greater than Yom Kippur, and the place that witnesses it holier than the Holy of Holies." Quoted by André Lacocque and Pierre-Emmanuel Lacocque, *Jonah: A Psycho-Religious Approach to the Prophet,* 140. Compare Luke 15.7, "There is more rejoicing in heaven over one sinner who repents than over ninety-nine righteous who need no repentance." Not all versions of the story include Ninevite repentance, however. In the second-century BCE book of Tobit, the aged Tobit ad-

vises his son to leave Nineveh because Jonah has (presumably accurately) predicted its destruction. The version told by Josephus in *Antiquities of the Jews,* published in late first century CE, concludes with Jonah praying for and receiving pardon for his sins, prophesying the destruction of Nineveh, which Josephus has said did occur, and returning home. In the Koran, both Jonah and the Ninevites become exemplars of faith.

9. See Louis Ginzburg, *The Legends of the Jews,* 246–253. The Lacocques see Nineveh as both a symbolic Sodom and the eighth-century BCE equivalent of Nazi Germany. They argue, however, that the book of Jonah satirizes post-exilic theocracy and exclusivist nationalism: "The restoration [of Israel], intimates the author of Jonah, will occur only *with* the nations, not without them" (126–127). Jack M. Sasson, among others (*The Anchor Bible: Jonah, A New Translation with Introduction, Commentary, and Interpretation,* 274), observes that "Jonah's alleged incapacity to share God's love with anyone who is not a Hebrew has unfortunately become a metaphor [among Christian commentators] by which to censure Judaism"—despite the fact that the text is itself a Jewish one in which Jonah is being criticized, while numerous Jewish commentaries emphasize that the Ninevites, like the Israelites, are God's handiwork. Sherwood discusses anti-Jewish readings of Jonah, 21–32.

10. Rabbi Jonathan Magonet, *Whither Shall I Go From Your Spirit: A Study of the Book of Jonah,* 11.

11. Jacqueline Osherow has pointed out that Jonah omits from his version of the litany the word *emet,* truth. "Cleft in the Rock/Engraved in Stone: God's Glory from the Other Side," paper presented at Association of Writers and Writing Programs, Austin, Texas, April 2005.

12. Of all twentieth-century authors, Beckett may be the closest to the spirit of the author of the Book of Jonah in his sense of absurdity. In his "Act Without Words I: A Mime for One Player," the scene is "Desert. Dazzling light." A man is flung onstage, attempts to leave, is flung back, several times. A tree with a single bough descends from above to shade him, then its fronds close and the shade vanishes. See Samuel Beckett, *Breath and Other Shorts* (London: Faber and Faber, 1971), 23–29.

13. See the Lacocques' *Jonah,* xviii and passim, on the "Jonah complex," and their diagnosis of Jonah as "an acutely depressed person," 88. See also Abraham Maslow, *Toward a Psychology of Being,* on "the Jonah syndrome," and A. D. Cohen, "The Tragedy of Jonah," 164–175: "Jonah's behavior represents a clear clinical picture of despair and, more fundamentally, of depression."

14. Sigmund Freud, "Humour," *Abstracts,* 163.

Job: The Open Book

1. My thanks to Jill Hammer and to Mary Campbell (personal correspondence) for pointing out significant instances when the theme does arise. In an Egyptian liturgical hymn, for example, Isis says: "It is I who made justice stronger than wealth, and I who designed penalties for evil. It is I who first created mercy and I who mete it out." In the myth of Osiris, the god abolished cannibalism, civilized the known world, became the judge of the dead, and was seen in essence as the god of goodness. Concepts of justice do not, however, seem to dominate pre-Judaic religions as they do Judaism. Judeo-Christian concepts of justice are what western civilization inherits, along with Roman ideas which are essentially secular.

2. See Elaine Pagels, *The Origin of Satan,* 41–42.

3. C. J. Jung, *Answer to Job,* 13ff. Jung is one of the very few commentators on the Book of Job who is prepared to argue that Job is morally superior to his Maker and, further, that Yahweh is a "despot" driven by passions of which he himself is unconscious. A similar reading is that of Jack Miles, *God: A Biography.* In Archibald Macleish's play *J. B.,* Satan is understood to be an aspect of God.

4. After three rounds of accusation and counteraccusation, a new speaker enters, the youth Elihu, who expresses impatience at the three friends for not convincing Job, and then goes into a harangue which is no more convincing than theirs. Most commentators see this passage (32–37) as a later addition to the book, by an inferior hand.

5. Martin Buber, *The Prophetic Faith,* 191.

6. Several ancient parallels to Job exist, including an Egyptian "Protest of the Eloquent Peasant" dating from the twenty-first century BCE, which concerns a cheated man complaining to a local official, and a Sumerian poem of the early second millennium BCE, in which an upright man afflicted by a severe illness prays to his god and desires his family to join him, but he finally confesses that he has sinned—at which point the god exorcises his demon. The most famous parallel is a poem known as "The Babylonian Job," in which a high-ranking man, stricken with a terrible malady which he laments for a year, is finally cured after dreaming that Marduk sends messengers to perform rites of exorcism. In none of these works is there an accusation of deities.

7. See Robert Sutherland, *Putting God on Trial: the Biblical Book of Job,* for a discussion of the role of the parallel monsters in Babylonian and Canaanite mythology, and for the apocalyptic imagery associated with them in Isaiah and in later Jewish legend.

8. For a variety of arguments regarding Job's final words, see David Robertson, "The Book of Job: A Literary Study," 446–469; Stephen Mitchell, *The Book of Job,* xxv–xxvii, xxxii; Edwin M. Good, *In Turns of Tempest: A Reading of Job,* 371; Miles, *God,* 322–325, 425–430.

9. I recommend to readers the exercise of asking acquaintances who believe the Bible to be "literally" true, to show them some of its contradictions and ask them which version of the story is the true one.

10. I thank Diana Lipton for pointing out to me that the Book of Job has found no place in Jewish liturgy, unlike every other text discussed in this book, including even Ecclesiastes, and that its cantillations are said to be impossible to perform.

11. See Michael Walser, *Exodus and Revolution.*

12. Harold Schweizer, *Suffering and the Remedy of Art,* 73.

13. My fantasy regarding Job's wife is in *The Nakedness of the Fathers: Biblical Visions and Revisions,* 235–240. The experience of having this fantasy in the fall of 1986 triggered the wrestling with the Hebrew Bible and Jewish tradition I have subsequently undertaken. Several passages in the present chapter are lifted from that book.

14. Jung, *Answer to Job,* 9–10, 42–43, 66.

15. Miles, *God,* 11.

16. Jack Miles, *Christ: A Crisis in the Life of God,* 12.

17. Quoted as epigraph to Michael Lerner, *Jewish Renewal: A Path to Healing and Transformation.*

18. Yehuda Amichai, *Selected Poetry,* 1.

19. Yehuda Amichai, *Open Closed Open,* 113.

Afterword

1. Gerald L. Bruns, "Midrash and Allegory: the Beginning of Scriptural Interpretation," in Alter and Kermode, *The Literary Guide to the Bible,* 633.

Alicia Suskin Ostriker is a prize-winning poet and critic, whose work appears in many Jewish anthologies and journals. Her previous writing on the Bible includes *The Nakedness of the Fathers: Biblical Visions and Revisions* (Rutgers University Press) and the Preface to an edition of *The Five Scrolls*. Ostriker is professor emerita of Rutgers University.